T0380808

BETWEEN THE LINES

Minister Bill

WESTBOW
PRESS®
A DIVISION OF THOMAS NELSON
& ZONDERVAN

WestBow Press books may be ordered through booksellers or by contacting:

WestBow Press
A Division of Thomas Nelson & Zondervan
1663 Liberty Drive
Bloomington, IN 47403
www.westbowpress.com
1 (866) 928-1240

ISBN: 978-1-9736-1258-2 (sc)
ISBN: 978-1-9736-1257-5 (e)

Print information available on the last page.

WestBow Press rev. date: 1/2/2018

ABOUT THE AUTHOR

Minister Bill has been a member of a Missionary Baptist Church for more than sixty-five years. He served in numerous capacities in an effort to help the church better serve the Kingdom of God. He served in the youth ministry, transportation ministry, business manager and treasurer, and for over twelve years in the deacon ministry. He was ordained as a Minister of the gospel by the National Organization of Ministers in the year 2015. He often states that he is just a nobody trying to tell everybody about the Saving Power of Christ Jesus. Two of his favorite sayings are (you make me smiles with my heart) and (can you imagine how much I love you). The degree of joy given him can only come from God. The Love that he has for God takes a very strong imagination. Minister Bill believes the primary purpose of religion is to help people live life more abundantly by forming a loving relationship with our Heavenly Father through Jesus Christ.

A BETTER UNDERSTANDING OF GOD'S MESSAGE

For more than 65 years I have been a member of a Baptist church that is now 125 years old. For more than 12 years I served as a deacon. I have listen to a thousand sermons and read thousands of words. I have never heard a preacher question anything written in the bible. Most churches believe that the bible is word perfect. If they do not, they will not say it. They believe that God inspired the writing of Scripture. For this reason, it must be perfect. The perfection of the bible is a must for those who believe the primary purpose of the bible is to show the world that God is perfect. For those who believe the primary purpose of the bible to be inspiration, word perfection is secondary. The primary purpose of the bible is to help us better understand the message of God. This book was written for that purpose. Christianity is a faith. No one can prove another wrong. God gave us brains to use. If we do not use them, it is an insult to Him. My heart and brain tell me to believe and trust in God, Jesus, and the Holy Ghost. Nothing else is perfect.

There are some who will think that this book is a criticism of the bible. It is not. I am not a critic. A critic is one who knows the price of everything and the value of nothing. I know the value of the bible. The bible is an excellent book of faith. If there is any criticism, it is directed to the misunderstanding of the primary purpose of the bible. Only God and Jesus are perfect. The pure at heart will see God. When we know Jesus, we have seen God. Any one and any statement that in any way lessens the Divine Nature of Jesus the Christ should be criticized. Nothing known to man is perfect other than God, Jesus, and the Holy Ghost.

The purpose of this book is to provide a deeper understand of God's word, to come to reality with God's message, INSPIRATION.

Minister Bill

READING BETWEEN THE LINES

We read Scripture. We listen to bible readers who call themselves teachers. We would like to accept their understanding as being correct without question. That's the problem, without question. You hear the same reasoning over and over again to the point that you start to accept it as being correct. Could it be a wrong way of looking at it? Not only could it be a wrong way of looking at it, but, it could be completely incorrect. Where in the bible will you find the quote (God helps them that help themselves)? You won't. It is not in the bible. Yet, we have heard it so many times that we start to believe that it is a part of Scripture. There is another old saying (believe none of what you hear and only half of what you see). The point is, stop taking other people's word for it and start reading between the lines.

How much faith do you have in Jesus? Do you believe that He is the Son of God? How then can you believe that His human will could over power His spiritual will? How then can you believe that He would say (Father, why have you forsaken me?). The apostle John was there at the foot of the Cross. You will not be able to find this quote in his gospel. What did Jesus actually mean by saying (Father forgive them for they know not what they do)? Did the Jewish leaders know what they were doing when they decided to kill Jesus? They followed Him. They saw His miracles. They knew that no natural human being could do what He did. They saw Him feed thousands with almost nothing. They saw Him give life to those who had died. Jesus told them many times, if you don't believe Me, believe that which you have seen. You will have some teachers of scripture tell you that the Jewish leaders believed that Jesus was disobeying the laws of Moses. Was that their primary reason? Or was their primary reason for getting rid of Jesus the fact that it was in their self-interest to do so. I am the Chief Priest. The leader of the Jews. No one is going to take-a-way my followers. No one is going to stand in front of my followers and call me a hypocrite. I'm going to get him. And they did? He is the son of Joseph and I'm not going to believe anything else.

Jesus was a kind and compassionate person. Could this be the reason He asked His Father to forgive them? Did He actually mean, forgive their lack of belief? There are some evil people in this world. People who hurt even kill others because they like the feeling. People who would not ask for forgiveness on their death bed. Some believe that they will be forgiven because Jesus died for our sins. Others believe that if you do not seek forgiveness, ask the Father for forgiveness, you will not receive it. Repentance. Without it you will be forever lost.

SCRIPTURE

One of the biggest mistakes that man has made is putting the word holy in front of the word bible. God inspired the writing of the original Scripture. He did not inspire that which happen to the Word after it was written. All things that man has touched is infected. That includes the bible. There are those who believe that the bible is word perfect. It has to be because it was inspired by God. Moses and Abraham were inspired by God, yet, they made mistakes. Being inspired by God does not mean that you will be perfect. Someone got it wrong. Did Jesus say (Father take this cup from me). Or did He ask the question (should I ask You to take this cup from Me?) Then answer His own question by saying (NO, the fulfillment of this cup is the reason for my journey.) Were His last words, (Father why have You forsaken Me). Or, (Father, unto You I commit My Spirit). Or, (It is finished). Who was at the Crucifixion to hear witness the last words of Jesus? The bible does not tell us that Matthew, Mark or Luke were there. It does tell us that John was there. You will not find this quote in the gospel of John. Scripture was subject to error because it was written by humans who were not perfect.

Who decided what writings would be a part of the bible and what would not? Was it a Divine force or the decision of man? Why are there 73 Books in the Catholic bible, but, only 66 in the Protestant bible? Man, not God, made the judgment as to what they wanted you to read. There were 80 Books in the King James translation of 1611. We are reading only that which man has decided is not dangerous or heretical to Christianity. We have not been permitted to make that decision for ourselves.

Emperor Constantine, in 312 A.D. put Christianity on an equal footing with all other religions. That is all he did that was favorable to Christianity. He believed that the church and State should work closely together. He eliminated Jewish religious practices and that which the disciples of Christ had established in the early church. He changed the day of worship and rest from the 7th day Saturday to the 1st day Sunday. His Reformation of Christianity fragmented the wisdom of history.

The Roman Catholic church did not want people to have bibles. Church leaders were afraid that if people could read the Word for themselves, they would stop accepting them as God's chosen and stop bringing their monies to church. King James and the church did not get along. He, after having the bible translated into English, forced the church to make the bible available to the people. There is believed to be close to 600 Books of scripture. Catholic church leaders decided that only 73 should be included in the bible. Protestant leaders decided that only 66 Books would be a part of the bible. Those who think that man has not had a negative effect on Scripture are fooling themselves.

UNDERSTANDING THE BIBLE

Much is written about the bible because it is the most important written document that Christians have. It is an excellent history book. It is an excellent book of inspiration. Those are the two primary purposes of the bible. It does not have to be completely accurate to fulfill those two primary objectives.

Christians should accept the bible for it's true purposes. The bible can be difficult to understand. Two different people can read the same Scripture and see different messages. One can read the bible more than once and get understanding from a scripture that they did not get from previous readings. There is no way to prove if these understandings are correct meaning the same as those who wrote the scripture. The only thing that is certain, without question, is that there is a God and Jesus is His Son.

There are some who believe that the bible is absolutely accurate word for word. God made it that way. There are others who believe that God inspires man, but, God does not perfect man. Therefore, anything touched by man has been infected. Could not be perfect because there has been only one perfect person who ever walked this earth, Jesus. The bible was not written by Jesus. Jesus was a Jew, not a Christian. There are others who will state that you must accept all of the bible or none of it. How could you know what to believe and what not to believe? Why did God give you a brain? You know no human is perfect. All men make mistakes. Does that mean that you will not believe anything a person might say? God gave you a brain to think and reason. Jesus did not once tell you that the bible would be printed and that you should worship it. Jesus told you to worship God and accept Him as the Son of God. Your confidence should be in God and Jesus. Everything else, including the bible, is secondary. Yes, you might be wrong in your understanding of certain scriptures. Yes, your bible teacher might be wrong. But, that doesn't matter if your trust and faith is where it should be. Right on God and Jesus.

There are reasons to realize that all English scripture could not be completely accurate. Understanding that much of scripture is here say. Where did Mark and Luke get their information? There were translation problems from Hebrew and Greek into English. This includes the character of the translators. The bible, like all books of faith, tell us only that which others want us to believe.

Is it necessary to read the bible to believe in God and Jesus? Billions of people believed far before the bible was available. People who cannot read at all have in the past and do in the present believe. Man cannot have an effect on the Trinity. Believe in God, Jesus, and the Holy Spirit.

FOLLOWERS OF JESUS

You go to church on Sunday. You sing pretty songs of praise. You Amen and get emotional. Then you go home after church and turn on the television. You live in a comfortable home and you drive a nice car. But, that's not enough. You want a bigger home and a more luxurious car. Where are your priorities? You like to look and feel important. You want others to think that you have made it. Are you sure you are a follower of Jesus or just a cheerleader! You pray for others, but, do you do anything to help those who you pray for? You go to church on Sunday, but, do you offer your time and talents to help your church better accomplish its mission? You believe you are Saved, but, are you really all you should be?

You claim to have faith, but, what good is faith if you have no deeds? Genuine faith in God should always result in action that demonstrate that faith. You are saved by faith, but, if faith is alone, it is not faith. Do you think God will believe anything? He will test you to see if you are sincere. It is true that we will not receive our rewards for our good deeds in this life. It is true that our good works will not help get us into heaven. Only the Grace of God will do that. But, Scripture tells us that Jesus will reward us for our good works. This reward can only come after we get to heaven. You will receive the degree of JOY you deserve for your efforts to promote the Kingdom of God while you are here on earth.

Your priorities must change. You must learn from the Master Chef if you are to be a true follower of Jesus. The bible tells you exactly what God expects of you. It will cost you something to follow Jesus. (and whoever wants to be first must be slave to all). If you really want to be a follower of Jesus, you must be willing to do the Will of Jesus. Feed the hungry, cloth the naked, visit those who are in prison. What good is it for a man to gain the world and lose his Soul? You cannot serve both God and money. When you begin to help others without thinking about it, you have arrived. When doing good becomes a habit, you will know that the Holy Spirit is within you. That's what Jesus was all about. Doing good. Helping people. As a true follower of our Savior, that's what you should be all about. You will only find peace and be truly blest when you give Him your body and Soul.

HE DIED FOR OUR SINS

How many times have you heard this said? He died for our sins. Has anyone explained what they mean? This could not mean that humans will do longer commit sinful acts. They do that every day. Does it mean that you will be forgiven for your sins automatically? Some believe this to be true. Do You? Considering the condition of the world two thousand years after Jesus, we can come to the following conclusions. Jesus has defeated sin and thus Satan. Satan knows this, but, he is a die hard. He wants to prevent everyone he can from enjoying the Victory given to us by Jesus. When we put on the armor of Jesus each morning, we are protected from the evil temptations of the devil. When he sees the armor you have on, he will leave and find someone with less protection. That is one way that Jesus helped us by His death on the Cross. We are better able to resist the evil temptations of Satan. Sometimes the devil will win a battle, but, he can never win the war against a person who has love for Jesus. When you do sin, God will forgive you if you ask for forgiveness with a sincere heart. Repent. Your heart must be sincere. God will be able to tell. God's forgiveness is another way Jesus helped us by His death on the Cross. David committed many very bad sins. The reason it is said that David was a man after God's own heart, is because he went to God each time and sincerely asked for forgiveness. You do not have to be perfect to satisfy God. He knows you are human. He knows you are a sinner. He knows if you are doing your best to resist sin. He knows your heart.

Oh, if only more people would understand and take advantage of the Victory Jesus has given us. It would be like taking food out of the devil's mouth. He would starve to death. It is a fact that people who believe in God and Jesus commit fewer crimes, fewer sins, compared to people who do not believe. It is a fact that believers commit less serious crimes, sins, than people who do not believe. People who attend church regularly are not perfect. But, they have a force deep within that helps keep them on the straight and narrow. Regular attendance is necessary because human beings are weak. They need reinforcement regularly. Jesus has done so much for us we cannot tell it all. He did not have to die on the Cross. God does not force anyone to do anything. Jesus told us numerous times that He had the power to give His life and the power to take it away. Jesus agreed to suffer and die because it was the Will of God and because of His love for both God and us. How can we tell if the love of God is within us? We have been told to test ourselves to ensure that the Holy Spirit is truly working within our hearts. When you look in the mirror and say with a smile on your face that nothing in this world is more important to you than the love of God. Not even life itself. You are willing to die, with a smile on your face, for God because Jesus, the Son of God, died for you. That is when you will know that your all has been laid on the altar.

WHAT DO YOU BELIEVE?

There are many religions. Many faiths in which we can believe. Hinduism, Islam, Judaism, Buddhism. Some are a lot older than Christianity. Every major religion has printed material telling why their belief is the right one. Islam calls it the Quan'an. Judaism calls it the Torah. Christianity calls it the bible. Every one of them will tell you that their writings are God inspired. There is an exception. Buddhism does not believe that there is a God. I don't know how they think all of these non-human made parts of this earth got here. I do not know how Muslims can believe in Islam when they know the background of Muhammad who was a person promoting death and destruction. Judaism, from be beginning, believed that they did not need a savior to save them from sin. Many now believe differently.

The Quan'an, the Torah, the bible, are they all God inspired? Are none of them God inspired? Ask your pastor the following question. Jesus said no one come to the Father but through Me. Will only Christians be saved? Everyone else who believes in God, but, not Jesus will be left out. They will go somewhere, but, not to heaven. Your pastor will base his answer on the bible. You are putting your trust in the believes of someone else. On what does the pastor base her/his belief? If a Christian, it must be the bible. Who wrote the bible? Was it written by human beings just as was the Quan'an and Torah. It was translated by human beings. Was it infected by human beings just as the others?

You have read the New Testament. Where in the New Testament does Jesus tell you to believe in every word written in the bible? Where does He prophesy the coming of the bible? Jesus tells us to spread the Good News by evangelism. Direct communication person to person. Direct communication preacher to congregation which is actually a direct form of evangelism. Can a person who has never seen the bible believe in Jesus? There are hundreds of languages into which the bible has not been translated. There are people who only understand words in their language who believe in Jesus. Pastors have to stop telling their congregations that their belief is based on the bible. Their belief must be based on God and His Son Jesus. The bible is a Good Book. A good book of inspiration. We don't worship the bible. We worship God.

OVER ANALYZING SCRIPTURE

When we read scripture, we must remember the two C's, content and customs. It is possible that those translating scripture made numerous mistakes because they got the content wrong. The meaning of the word trunk cannot be certain without consideration of content. There are simply too many possibilities. Content considerations can become complex. When reading the Beatitudes, we might think that no person can live up to those standards. We must understand content. Jesus was speaking in a perfect state. He even stated that we should be perfect just as our Father in heaven is perfect. Jesus knew that it is impossible for a human being to be perfect. He made the statement because He wants us to reach for perfection. That is the only way we can become all that we can be. We are not sinners because we sin. We sin because we are sinners. Jesus knew we could not uphold all stated in the Beatitudes. That does not mean that we have no opportunity to enter God's kingdom. Jesus said, anyone who breaks one of the least of these Commandments will be called least in the kingdom. He here is stating that all is not equal in heaven. The amount of JOY received in heaven will not be the same for everyone. You might have an efficiency apartment instant of a luxury suite, but, you will still be in heaven.

Jesus said, except for marital unfaithfulness, anyone who divorces their mate commits adultery. Does this mean that a person being constantly abused by their mate should stay in the relationship? Of course not. Jesus loves you and wants you to love yourself enough to pack your bags when necessary. Remember, Jesus often spoke in the perfect state. We have to stop over analyzing scripture. We have to stop taking one statement and thinking it applies to all situations. An example of this is the statement, if you believe in the Son of God and believe in His Resurrection, you shall be saved. Does it say that you have to do nothing else? What about repentance? What about living your life in a Godly manner?

Each generation has customs. Many of which have been handed down from previous generations. Much of Paul's writings were influenced by customs. Paul stated that a woman should not speak in church. If she has questions, she should ask her husband when they get home. What would today's church look like without the voice of women? Customs even had an effect on statements made by Jesus. Do you actually believe that Jesus would support black people being held in a state of slavery today? Yet, scripture indicates that Jesus accepted slavery as part of Jewish life. There has never been a National law in the United States stating that it was lawful to hold blacks as slaves. Customs had to be broken.

In reading scripture, we must understand the kind of man and Divine Spirit Jesus is. With this understanding, we can safely apply the writings of the bible to our lives.

MAN'S INFLUENCE ON THE WORD of GOD

We would like to think that every word given to us in the bible is exactly as was spoken. It is not. Man has had a negative influence on God's Word from the beginning of his writings. Translators of the writings could not find English words to define some words written in Hebrew, Greek, or Arabic. Their decisions as to the words used were often influenced by their own believes. The civilization of Babylon stained God's Word to a great degree. The word Sunday comes from the worshippers of the sun not of God. God made the seventh day Holy, not the first day. Man changed God's Word. You are going to church on the devil's day, not the Lord's day. The people of Babylon also worshipped fire and the devil on Sunday. Worshippers of the sky, the rainbows.

In the King James version of the bible, the phrase Holy Ghost was used over ninety times. The phrase Holy Spirit was use only seven times. Why is it in later versions the term Holy Ghost was almost completely replaced with Holy Spirit? Why is it that the word fear is given a different meaning only when it is stated in the bible? Who told them that God wants people to feel comfortable with Him? We have to stop changing God's Word to our own level of comfort. Ask you pastor why human beings suffer. God does not give us the answer then how could your pastor have the correct answer? Have you ever heard of pastor say, I don't know? We have to take God at His Word. We have to stop changing God's Word to our likeness. God has told was that homosexuality is detestable. God don't play that. Yet, many churches do not follow the Word of God. Does your church make it clear that marriage between those of the same sex promotes homosexuality which is a sin before God?

Man has, from the beginning of his writings, done that which is detestable by trying to make God's Word what man wanted it to be. It was not meant to be easy to live a life to the standards of God.

BETWEEN THE LINES

In the course of learning more about the Word of God and His Son Jesus the Christ, we must attempt to get as much understanding from scripture as possible. This means that we must read between the lines. Understand that the bible was written by man. Man, inspirited by God, but, not perfected by God. Many writings have been influenced by man both with and without intention. We must accept that customs of the day have had an influence on writings both then and now. Of course, God does not agree that a human being should be beaten with a rod. We must read scripture with understanding. God gave you a brain and He expects you to use it.

We must be careful what we tell children. Mommy, where does God live? Where will I go when I die? Our immediate answer might be heaven. But, how could God live in heaven when the first sentence of the bible reads, "In the beginning, God created the heavens and the earth". This tells us that God was somewhere before the heavens were created. Scripture also tells us that, "heaven and earth will pass away, but, my words will never pass away". Heaven could not be eternity. Are you sure you want to go to a place that will pass away?

Where will we go when we leave here? There were many, in the days when Jesus walked the earth, who believed there was no Resurrection. The Sadducees believed when you die that was it. Many also believe this today. We cannot prove them wrong. We only have our faith. "Because you will not abandon me to the grave, nor will you let your Holy One see decay." There are many who believe that only the good will be raised from the grave. Not the good, bad, and ugly. Scripture tells us, "Multitudes who sleep in the dust of the earth will awake, some to everlasting life, others to shame with everlasting contempt" "…just as Christ was raised from the dead through the glory of the Father, we too may live a new life."

BETWEEN the LINES (2)

But what about now? I go to church almost every Sunday. I see all of these people who never go to church or open a bible or even believe in God. Look how good they live. Look at that car. I will never have a car like that. We must be honest with ourselves. If there were no Resurrection, how would it have an effect on the way you live? Would you still be as steadfast in the Word of the Lord? Is one of the reasons you do what you do because you are hoping for God's physical blessings in this life? Nothing is wrong with being jealous. "I am a jealous God." We must test ourselves to see if the love of God exceeds both our wants and needs. We must understand that this life is secondary to God. That is a hard statement to accept. We must also accept that the bad and the ugly may not receive, in this life, what is coming to them. But, it is coming. The Lord will punish men for all sins. God will bring every deed into judgment.

We must keep trying to do the right thing. That is a test of our faith and without faith it is impossible to please God. Being human, our faith might grow weary, God knows we are human. However, He does see the distinction between the righteous and the wicked. Those who serve God and those who do not.

BETWEEN the LINES (3)

What is the difference between Grace and Mercy? What is the difference between being a slave to God and being a slave to a human being? With both, we are at the grace and mercy of the master. The difference can be found in the meaning of the word love. God is demanding. He has told us that He will not take seconds. Either He is first in our lives or we are not worthy of Him. He will test us to find out if we are sincere. The test might not always be in the form of suffering. Suffering does not always come as a result of sin. No man has the right to question God regardless of the difficulties. We sometimes look at other people and wonder why we should suffer when it seems that God is letting others get-a-way with sin after sin. We find ourselves questioning God's ways. We were not meant to understand all of God's ways. Don't compare yourself to the other fellow. Stay out of God's territory. He has told you that He does not need or want your input. He does not need you telling Him how to do His job. He is God all by Himself.

A person who misses the way of wisdom may be as good as dead, even though he is still walking around. Wisdom includes knowing your place with your Heavenly Father. There is a way that seems right to man, but, will end in death. God's way is the only way. Scripture tells us, "No eye has seen, no ear has heard, no mind has conceived what God has prepared for those who love him". True love for your Father means complete trust in His way.

BETWEEN the LINES (4)

What has God prepared for those who love Him? We are told to live primarily for that which we cannot conceive. Don't do what you enjoy unless it is within the Graces of God. You don't know what your reward will be. All you have is His promise. Your primary goal in life is to prepare yourself to live for eternity with God. You don't have any details, but if it is with God, it has to be good. Death is not God's Will. That's one reason for Jesus coming to us. He has overcome death. Scripture tells us, "For my Father's will is that everyone who looks to the Son and believes in him shall have eternal life, and I will raise him up at the last day". Jesus will appear again, not to bear sin, but, to bring Salvation to those who believe in Him.

Jesus was born to die. To die for a reason. Because you are a sinner. It is your nature to sin. You must live your whole life in a war against Satan, against sin. The death of Jesus gave you the armor needed to win your battle with the devil. We have the Victory because of the life, death, and Resurrection of our Redeemer. Life is like playing a game that you know you have already won. Satan might win a few battles, but, Jesus has already won the war and the devil can go where he belongs. Hades.

It feels good to be Saved. To believe in Jesus. To believe that the best is yet to come.

BETWEEN the LINES (5)

By reading between the lines, we have found out that upon the second coming of Christ everyone in the grave will come out. Not just the good, but, also the bad and ugly. But, not everyone will go to live with God. Jesus will make that decision based on the way you have lived your life. Does that mean that only believers will be saved? Why does scripture read "…especially those who believe"? Scripture makes it clear that those who believe will receive first consideration. We must remember God said He will have mercy on whom He will have mercy. Will God have mercy on non-believers? It is better to depend on the Grace of God than His mercy alone. We have to believe in our hearts, confess with our mouths, have faith in our God, repent of our sins, and we have to prove all this by our deeds.

Ignorance of the law is no excuse, or is it? You could go to jail even if you didn't mean to do it. Is this also God's law? He is a merciful God. He will give you more than one chance to get it right if your heart is right. Don't think for a minute that His patience will not run out. There are curses for disobedience. He will not be with those who disobey His Will and His Ways. He will always have the door open for you to return to His good graces.

Fear the judgment of the Lord. Fear can be good. It can keep you out of harm's way. Scripture tells us to fear God and give Him glory, because the hour of His judgment has come. Arrogant and evildoers will be stubble and set on fire. But, for those who reverse His name, the sun of righteousness will rise with healing in tis wings.

BETWEEN the LINES (6)

We have been told to get ready and stay ready. This is not a part-time job. The Lord wants us to live each day of our lives like it is the last day and keep growing in His Spirit like we will live forever. You are not permitted to let your guards down for one day. That is all Satan is waiting for. No one knows the hour that God will call your name. Getting ready and staying ready is a cost of following Jesus. It takes work. If we do not take up the Cross and follow Jesus, we are not worthy of Him. One of the reasons you are so steadfast in the Word is self-interest. You want God's blessings in this life. You want to go live with Him in heaven. Self-interest is a part of human nature. We must ask ourselves are there any self-interest factors more important than our love for God. Nothing can separate us from the love of God. Can the same be said of our love for Him? The death and Resurrection of Jesus ensured us that we will never be separated from God. We will always have a direct relationship with Him. This signified access to God could have only been made by Jesus.

God has a right to be demanding. We have been bought with a price. The suffering of Jesus. Your life is not your own. We must fight Satan every day of our lives. He never sleeps. He will attack you even while you sleep. He will take over your life if you do not stop him. The only offensive weapon that we have is the sword of the Holy Spirit. Amazing enough, that is all we need. The devil knows he has lost the war. He is a die hard. He wants to keep as many as possible from enjoying the Victory of Jesus. Some are so spiritually weak that they will let Satan take them over. We are so glad that long ago we made Jesus our choice.

BETWEEN the LINES (7)

God has told us exactly what is required of us. Act justly, love mercy, and walk humbly. There is a degree of selfishness within the character of each of us. We wonder why God would even consider granting mercy to non-believers after requiring that we follow His Commandments. His mercy to others has no effect on us. We should be the kind of people who will follow the Commandments of God regardless of others. So why do we take a negative attitude toward the good received by others? How does it help you to speak negatively about another person? We often wonder why those who do wrong seem to prosper. We must be careful to act justly and have faith in God's judgment.

God told us exactly what is expected of us. Love the Lord with all your heart, soul, mind, and strength. Notice the order of this statement. He starts with the heart because it is the center of a person giving direction to all decisions. Next is the Soul where God lives within us. Third is the mind. Humans might give the mind a higher position, but, not God. The mind reacts to the heart. Finally, strength. Physical strength has nothing to do with it. The strength that is of importance is within given to us through the Holy Spirit. We will receive inter-strength only if we ask God for it. God's angels will also be with us. The devil is weak. He can do no more than we permit him to do. He knows who has the authority to drive him out. Scripture tells us, "He even gives orders to evil spirits and they obey him".

What an awesome God we serve.

BETWEEN the LINES (8)

Between the lines mean reading for understanding. It is true that God inspirits people, but, He does not perfect people. Throughout the written Word, men have infected God's Word for the purpose of putting his own slant on things. Sometimes unintentional and sometimes with intent. "God helps those who help themselves." We have heard this quote so many times that we begin to think it is from scripture. It is not in the bible. Where in the bible does it tell us that there were three wise men? Where in the bible does it tell us that an angel has a halo? Stop believing everything you hear or read. Man is not perfect, therefore, nothing that he writes or speaks is perfect. Man cannot have an effect on God, Jesus, or the Holy Ghost.

Human beings are hypocrites. One giving a false image. Unable to make his (inter) and (outer) life one. God is not fooled by appearances. This is important because we want to go to that place of perfect happiness and eternal communion with God. Salvation will come only by the Grace of God. Good works in this life will have no effect upon the judgment of Jesus Christ. But, our good works do have value. Jesus has stated that He will reward each person according to what that person has done. The JOY one receives in heaven will be administered by the way one has lived their life here on earth. Rewards in heaven and Salvation are not the same. God's degree of JOY will be our reward. Scripture reads,"…and that you. O Lord, are loving. Surely you will reward each person according to what he has done".

We serve a Just God.

BETWEEN the LINES (9)

Those who have tried to do more to promote God's kingdom while here on earth will receive more joy more reward when in heaven. Understanding received by reading between the lines tells us that all who pass through the pearly gates will not be equal. All will not receive the same degree of God's Joy. We learn that the good that we do not only has a positive effect on others, but, also on ourselves. We serve a Just God. He has told us that He will not forget the good that we have done to help His people.

God is the beginning and the end. "I AM that I AM" We all can say I am. This only means that we are here on this earth. We cannot truly say "That I AM". This means that my existence is in total my own. God is forever. Unlike you who will grow old, He is the same yesterday, today, and forever. Unlike you, He will never die. He started it all and He will end it all. He is God all by Himself. The Ruler of the Universe. We see all the horrible happenings around us. We think, how can a God of love and mercy permit this? We make the mistake of trying to figure out God. Father, it's your thing, do what you what to do.

As for me and my house, we will serve the Lord. We will love You Father with all our heart, soul, mind, and strength. We will say You are our Lord, our refuge our fortress in whom we will always trust. We will leave it to the smart ones to figure You out. All we what to do Father is love You. For You have been so good.

BETWEEN the LINES (10)

Do you believe that God wants you to be a slave to another human being? Is it not obvious that the customs of the times played a great role in the influence of the men who wrote scripture? Jesus told us that we will have trouble in this life. We pray and tell the Lord how big our troubles are. Maybe we should be telling our troubles how big our God is. The cruelty of Egyptian taskmasters turned the people of Israel against Moses who was sent to free them. We must not turn from Jesus who has come to free us. King Saul and Moses did not follow the instructions of the Lord. His way or your way. Trust His way. When the Lord gives you instructions, it is as important as that which He has told you to do. If it were not important, why do you think He would have given you the instructions? Following less than all the Commandments is still disobedience.

God demands a ransom for your life. You can pay the Lord with service. You will never be able to pay your debt off. The payment comes in the form of trying to live a life pleasing to God. Rich and poor are to give their all. Your reward in paradise will depend on your effort. God loves to be praised. He is a jealous God. God's test is so the fear of the Lord will be in you to keep you from sinning. You are a slave. A slave of righteousness. You are an heir to His Great Kingdom.

TRUST

I will trust in the Lord till I die. Do you think that trust is believing that God will make things right for you in this world? The Lord will make a way somehow. When we believe this, we are putting God to the test. God has nothing to prove to us. He has proven His love through Jesus. Jesus did not die in His sleep. He died a painful humiliating death. He suffered greatly to show God's love for us. Put your trust in things eternal. We have the misconception that the primary reason for Jesus is our existence in this life. One of the primary reasons the Jewish people let Jesus down is because they were more concern with their physical state of being under the Roman Empire than their spiritual state of being under God.

Are you the same way? Do you wonder why this race is so hard to run? Why good fortune always seems to pass you by? Are you more concerned with your state of being here in this life than your relationship with God? We often think, I try to do the right things. I try to live my life in a manner hopefully pleasing to God. Why can't I get a break? Why am I living from paycheck to paycheck knowing that if anything else bad happens, I'm in a world of trouble? You think you should be rewarded for doing the right thing.

News. Jesus did not come to earth for the primary reason of helping you feed your face. He came for the primary purpose of helping you to Save your Soul. Accept the fact that life is nothing more than a temporary assignment. Don't get too attached. You won't be here long.

SAFE AT HOME

Many time throughout the stages of our lives we feel that we are rounding third and headed for home. We finally stop thinking first about life in this world and we start giving some attention to our eternal life. Being Saved is a gift from God. We must all appear before the judgment seat of Christ, that each one may receive what is due him for the things done while in the body, whether good or bad. Anyone who does wrong will be repaid for his wrong, and there is no favoritism. Wait a minute. First, we are told that we are Saved by the Grace of God. Then we are told that we will be judged for that which we have done, good or bad. Which is it? Grace has nothing to do with that which we do. Or, does it? Do we actually think that our Just God is going to turn His back on our earthly actions? We might not understand it, but, God must have some standards with regard to His Grace. It is written that God is not unjust. He will not forget the love you have shown Him by helping His people. What are we to believe?

Today you will be with Me in paradise. This is what was said to the criminal who spoke up for Jesus while on the Cross. He was a criminal. A wrong doer. Yet, Jesus told him, he would go to paradise. Explain that if you can. Does that tell us that if your heart is right at death, your earthly actions do not matter? Does it really matter how we live our lives?

When your head touches your pillow tonight, are you satisfied that you touched all the bases as you rounded third and headed for home? Tomorrow was meant for some, but, tomorrow many never come. Did you fight a good fight, stay the course, keep the faith? Did you repent? Ask God for forgiveness of your sins. Did you try your best to live a life that is pleasing in the sight of God? If you did all of these things, you will be safe at home. Trust in God's goodness. He looks beyond your faults to see your needs. Forgiveness of sin is a need. Keep plenty of oil for your lamp. Hush, Hush, - Somebody is calling my name.

RICH (vs) WEALTH

Which would you rather have? Or, are they the same? Can a person have wealth without being rich? Can a person be rich without having a lot of money? Why is it that those who do the right thing so often seem to lose out, while those who take shortcuts, cheat, steal and lie seem to have the advantage? Be sure, your sins will find you out.

A lot of money makes a person wealthy not rich. Jesus stated that the love of money, not money itself, is the root of all evil. To love anything more than God is evil. God should be the Center of our Joy. When we lose realization of this, we lose all our riches regardless of how much wealth we have.

Jesus never made a sweeping indictment against wealth. Rather, He condemned the misuse of wealth. We lose sight of reality when we permit the ends for which we live to become confused with the means by which we live. Without dependence on God, our efforts turn to ashes and our sunrises into darkness. We become dead spiritually far before we die physically.

Are you rich? Rich in the love of God, family, and friends. All the money in the world cannot enrich your life as can the love of God. We will not find peace, love, and joy until we learn that a person's life does not consist of the abundance of possessions but in those inner treasuries of the Spirit.

When you look in the mirror, what do you see? Do you see a person rich in the love of God? If not, look again and keep on looking until you make God the Center of your Joy.

THE BIBLE

The bible makes no attempt to prove the existence of God. It begins by stating that in the beginning, God created heaven and earth. Einstein had a theory of general relativity. Are you only believing in a Jewish theory? Why did God make Jews His chosen people? Well, that is what the Jewish people tell us. If you believe in the bible, you believe in the supernatural. How can you expect an Atheists to believe in the supernatural?

God did inspire the writing of the bible. God inspired the original authors of scripture. God did not inspire the numerous versions and translations that followed. Once other men got hold of the original writings, those writings were infected by their prejudice and disbelief.

Some bibles are not entitled HOLY. Look at The Student and New International versions. You will have to read many words before you find the word HOLY. One of the biggest mistakes made by man is putting the word Holy in front of the word bible. Research the people King James chose to translate the bible. They were a lot less than all they should have been.

The bible was written for those who already believe. Non-believers could consider the bible science fiction. Every word in the version that you have is not the exact word as spoken. You must believe in miracles to believe in the bible. It is ok to believe in miracles. It is ok to believe in the supernatural. Believing in the birth of Jesus means that we believe in a Divine Marvel.

There are many good people in this world. People who would not hurt anyone. People who would do anything to help another. Many of whom never pick-up a bible. They will not give God the time of day much less accept Jesus as Lord of their lives. Will you see them in heaven? That's God's call. But as for me and my house, we will serve the Lord.

THE CHURCH

Most people don't go. Some say, when you die, you die. That's it. Some say, Catholic churches have so much gold hanging from their walls that you could not count it all and they still try to get people with lesser means, like me, to give them more. We can think of many reasons not to do anything. Some of those reasons have merit. Why did people like Paul, Timothy, and Titus devote their lives to the establishment of the church? Why did so many, starting with Jesus, give up their lives to spread the Good News throughout the world? It was once said that if a man has not found something worth dying for, he does not deserve to live. Jesus, Steven, Paul, Peter and many others found something worth dying for. The Salvation of God.

It is true that some people go to church for the wrong reasons. Scripture tells us that such people will not inherit the Kingdom of God. Others go to church for reasons like those people who go to a hospital. They need healing. Some are seeking forgiveness. Some feel closer to God. Some feel blessed and just want to give back. Some just want to praise His name. Some are seeking strength to carry on. Some have serious physically and mental conditions, like drug addiction, and realize that they cannot correct the problem on their own. Some just want to thank God for His goodness.

It helps to know that we don't have to live this life alone. God wants full control of your life, mind, body and Spirit. We need to seek a personal daily intimate loving relationship with Him. Being a strong church member is important. Living each day with God is even more important.

MARRIAGE, LOVE, SEX

Does God approve of a man having more than one wife? The Old Testament reviles people with more than one wife. That did not seem to be a concern of God. Marriage to a person who would come between a man and his relationship with his Heavenly Father was a concern. This is a reason so many marriages end up today in a court of law. How can there be understanding when the most important factor is not discussed prior to the wedding. What is your view point on God, Jesus, and a Christian life?

Sex is not important to older couples. Older couples seem to love each other even more. When you marry, your life is no longer your own. Every decision must be in equal consideration of another person. This could be the primary reason for divorce. A couple must have something in common. A love for God. This is the bond that is not seen, but, the bond that both people feel. A family that prays together stays together. When God is the Center of your family, your kids can see this and it is reflected in their behavior. When God is the Center of your family, your spouse treats you right and loves you even more. When God is the Center of your family, trouble don't last always. When God is the Center of your JOY, what others say about you doesn't matter. There is no bitterness, resentment, anger, anxiety or doubt. There is only hope, peace, wisdom, vision, patience, kindness, goodness, faithfulness, gentleness, and self-control. Knowing that your life is in the hands of the Creator of Heaven and Earth.

SMALL THINGS

Are there any clouds in God's beautiful sky today? We are so involved living in the fast lane that we forget to smell the roses. God created this beautiful earth because He wants us to enjoy it. Let he who has eyes see the wonders of God. We are looking at miracles. Our limitations help us to appreciate the small yet meaningful things in our everyday lives. It gives us more appreciation for the love and power of our Heaven Father.

Christians sometime think that they can save the world. Scripture tells was that there will be terrible times in the last days. People will be lover of themselves. Lovers of pleasure rather than lovers of God. The end of the Age has already been determined. You only have a limited number of years to write your name in the Book of Life. Talk to others about the wonders of God's world. The mission of Jesus Christ. Recognize and appreciate God's wonders. His greatest wonder is you. The Spirit is the place within you were God resides. Where you connect with God. His Spirit lives in you. Seek His voice and you will hear Him. He is speaking to you in both a loud strong voice and in a quiet soft voice. Be still and listen.

DO YOU TRUST THE BIBLE?

The bible is for those who already believe in God and believe that Christ Jesus is the Son of God. You must believe in miracles to believe in the bible. Jesus is a miracle. A miracle is an event that can only be attributed to a Divine or supernatural source. Jesus is Divine. No person like Him has ever walked this earth. The people who wrote scripture and the people who selected the writings to be made a part of the bible believed. All of the people who translated scripture into English might not have been believer. These translators were under the control of King James, not God. We will never know the honesty degree of their work.

It only takes one lie to make you a liar. All human beings are liars. There is not an adult human being who ever lived who has not told a lie. Who has not made a mistake. Think of the number of human hands the bible must have passed through before it was finalized. We cannot reasonably believe that the bible is without error.

The bible is not perfect. Composers of the bible selected only the writings that they agreed with. Does all of that really matter if you believe in Jesus? We praise Jesus, not the bible. Everything your pastor tells you on Sunday might not be exactly correct. Don't believe everything you read and hear. Believe in God, Jesus, and the Holy Ghost. Nothing else is perfect. Believe that God sent Jesus to us to let us know of His every lasting love. The bible does not have to be perfect for God, Jesus, and the Holy Ghost to be perfect. Be glad you got your religion in time.

CHRISTIANITY

No one said the road would be easy. There are over two billion Christians of the earth. Yet, when you count all the other faiths and those who have no faith, Christianity if in the minority. There are more people in this world who do not believe in Jesus the Christ than do. There is a difference between the Cross and Crucifix. A Crucifix you wear around your neck. The Cross you wear in your heart. There have been thousands that have suffered and died in the name of Christianity. There are countries today that will bring bodily hurt to those who follow Jesus. Christianity is in the minority and under attack in this world.

Some Christians are optimist. The doctrine that the universe is constantly tending toward a better state. There are enough riches in this world, but, because of selfish people, there will always be hunger and poverty. Christianity will never be able to bring all people to Christ. What's wrong with optimism? It seduces us into looking on the bright side at the risk of failing to take reality seriously. Optimism is not the rule. It is the exception to the rule. We cannot live in a state of exception.

So, what does Christianity have to offer if not optimism? A Gospel of Hope. God does not tell us that He will take away pain and suffering. He tells us that He will use distress to produce Hope. To produce GOOD. If it does not kill me, it will make me stronger. It might destroy my body, but, it will never destroy my Soul.

Christianity did not come into the world with a fixed silly grin on its face. It's hard love. Requiring vigorous mental and physical effort to do, understand, and explain. In fact, sometimes you cannot understand or explain it. That's were trust comes in. I will trust in the Lord till I die. Once you sincerely make that statement, you are a Christian.

CHRISTIAN JEWS

Jesus was not a Christian. He was a Jewish Rabbi. Christianity did not exist when Jesus walked this earth. Today it has developed into the largest faith in the world. Without the Jewish rejection of Jesus, there would be no Christianity. Even after the death of Jesus, Jews continued to reject Him by making it deathly to preach His Word. The Sadducees did not believe in Resurrection. Believers in Jesus had to go through many difficulties placed on them by Orthodox Jews. A Christian Jew is a person who believes in Jesus Christ. Some continue to read and trust the Torah, but, they do not believe in the Theological approach of Orthodox Jews. Some still believe that Jesus is not the only road to heaven.

A Christian Jew has been called by many names such as Hebrew Christians and Follower of the Way. The difference between Christian Jews and Orthodox Jews is the way they understand the Old Testament. Orthodox Jews understanding is limited to the Laws of Moses. Christian Jews understand that the New Testament is a (Revelation) of the Old Testament. It eliminates the limitations of the Torah. Christian Jews believe that God so loved the world that He gave His only Son that whoever believes in Him shall not perish but have ever lasting life with God and Jesus. I go to prepare a place for you for where I am there you shall be also.

KINGDOM FIRST

The Holy Spirit is powerful. It can change your mind. It can persuade you to do things beyond your wildest dreams. The Holy Spirit controls your heart. Your heart controls your mind and your mind control your body. The Holy Spirit will not keep you from committing sins. Your mind determines your decisions. The problem is that humans do not rely on the heart enough in making decisions. People do not let the Holy Spirit have complete control of their hearts.

The Holy Spirit only controls the heart if you want it to. God does not force Himself on anyone. Of primary importance to Jesus was doing the Will of God. He did not go through all that He did by force. Of primary importance to us should be doing the Will of God. That is part of the test. God wants to know that your will is His Will. The final decision was that of Jesus. The final decision is also yours.

We will be judged on what we do not on what we think or say. Sin is fun. If it were not, it would be easy to live a life free from sin. Sin is also temporary. Only a fool would accept temporary fun over eternal blessings. God does not condemn anyone. Humans condemn themselves. There are those who have chosen to be condemned. They continue to permit Satan to control their hearts and their actions.

You are an intelligent person. Put your actions on trial. Sit in judgment of the way you live. Who is in control of your heart? If it is not God, it is Satan. Satan enjoys taking over God's territory. He will lead you straight to hell if you let him. You know right from wrong. People who do wrong know right from wrong. By doing wrong, they are asking to make (Hades) their final home.

Just as the choice was that of Jesus, the choice is yours. Give your heart to Jesus. He won't take it unless you offer it. When you offer it, it will be the most satisfying day of your life. Is your all on the altar of sacrifice laid? Your heart does the Spirit control? You can only be blest and have peace and sweet rest as you give Him your body and Soul.

GOD's CHURCH (vs) SIN

The church is full of sinners. But, where is a better place for sinners to be than in church? God has put so much effort into establishing the church because He knows that without constant inspiration we will be far less than He wants us to be. The church is Holy Ground. God's house. We are only placed there to do His work. We take our orders from God. God has told us to stay away from evil doers. People who know right from wrong, yet, continue to do the devil's work. One can only learn right from wrong through teaching. God's church is responsible for this function by serving the community through the Holy Spirit.

Church members are there to help one another overcome their sins. The sinner must accept the fact that the life style they are living is not acceptable in the sight of God. People must repent. You will receive the forgiveness of God only if you seek it. We sinner must be taught to respect the Will of God. Church members must learn to treat every person as a child of God regardless of their sins. His Spirit can change your Soul.

Fornication, abomination, homosexuality, all sin has a place in God's church. That is the reason Jesus spent so much time with those who were spiritually sick. That is the reason Jesus said it is not the healthy who need a doctor, but, the sick. He did not come to call the righteous, but, sinners to repentance.

BE CAREFUL WHO YOU FOLLOW

Judaism came first. A main character was Moses. Christianity followed Judaism. The main character is Jesus. Islam followed approximately 500 years later. The man character was Muhammad. Today Christianity is the largest faith in the world with over two billion followers. Islam is second with approximately 1.5 billion followers. Both Christianity and Islam believe in God. The question is how can two faiths who both believe in God follow leaders who are so different?

Jesus believes in the love of one's neighbor. He never forced anyone to follow Him or demanded that His followers give Him money. He never ordered His follower to kill or physically hurt others. He never raped anyone. He related the message of God's love. He told us that God wants all people to love Him and each other.

Muhammad believed that anyone who was not a Muslim should be killed. Unbelievers should have their heads chopped off. Muslims should never befriend a Christian. Muhammad had 12 wives. He raped a nine-year old girl when he was age fifty. He demanded that his followers pay him 20% booty. Muhammad was a terrorist with primary interest in power, sex, and money.

Yet, there are over 1.5 billion people who believe Muhammad is the last Prophet sent by God. Who believe every word as stated in the Quran. Who disregard the fact that 123 verses in the Quran support war and death. Muslims do not believe that Jesus is the Son of God. They do not believe that He died on the Cross for our sins. They do not believe in Salvation.

False Prophets. As a child we learn that which we are taught. As an adult, one must start to examine the facts and think for one's self. Some things change. Some things never change. Our God of love could have never sent a person with the savage characteristics of Muhammad to represent Him. There will forever be billions of lost people in this world.

The decision is yours. Who will you follow? Love or hate? When you think of God, what kind of nature comes to mind? God is love. Jesus, His Son, give us the strong message of His love. Love your God with all your heart, Soul, mind, and strength. Your mind cannot conceive what God has prepared for those that love Him.

BAPTISM

A profession of faith. Proclaiming to the world that God directs your life and is more important to you than life itself. Christians are baptized in the name of the Father, Son, and Holy Ghost. The Trinity might not be simple to understand. The Trinity functions as One. The Holy Spirit can come to you anywhere, not just in church. Anywhere God determines that you are ready. You must be receptive. God does not force Himself on anyone. When we come out of the water, we are new beings filled with the Spirit of God and ready to live a new life. We are then spiritually ready to accept the Word and Love of God.

Some will say that they wish they were older before being baptized. That there is no way they could understand the meaning at such an early age. As a parent, you make decisions that you believe to be best for your child. Baptism is a head start in learning the Mystery of God's Word. Don't think for one minute that the Holy Spirit only comes to adults or people old enough to understand. It is a Mystery, and even as adults we will never fully understand. If your child wishes to be baptized a second time on the bases of spiritual understanding as an adult, this is perfectly acceptable.

God is a Mystery. We were not given life for the purpose of fully understanding God. We live to honor, praise, worship, and obey Him. God, unlike us, has no limitations. God sent Jesus to show us how to live to the Glory of God. Our Heavenly Father will decide if we have done our jobs.

FEAR of the LORD

We do not want to believe that God wants us to fear Him. We will find that many people change the word fear to a more comfortable word like respect. We don't feel comfortable with the term Holy Ghost. That is why many later versions of the bible has changed the term Holy Ghost to Holy Spirit. Does God want us to feel comfortable with Him or does God want us to accept, love and have respect for His position of authority over all things?

There are some factors that we do not want to accept. Fear is primary a source of control. Does God want to control us? He wants the Holy Ghost to live inside of us and direct our paths. We don't like the word slave. We think of it as a force of a person's will upon another. Yet, Paul stated the he is a slave of God. A voluntary slave of God. Do you fear the devil? Fear of him does not mean that you will run from him. It could mean that you will stand and fight to keep him out of your life.

We think of fear as a negative word. Should we fear the consequences of the judgment of God? The word fear was stated because it means exactly what it states. Fear of the Lord is the (beginning) of wisdom. It can develop into respect, reverence, and love. But, it is the beginning. Fear can be a good thing. As we learn more about God, fear will be over powered by love. God is LOVE.

I REALLY LOVE THE LORD

How much? How can you love someone you have never seen, yet, you don't love some who you have seen? Is one of the reasons you try to please God because you are seeking His blessing in the life? What's in it for me? All human beings are selfish to some degree. However, what are your priorities? God wants you to love Him above all else. Jesus said the love of even one's family should not exceed our love for Him.

Don't think for a moment that living a life that is pleasing to God is easy. You can't do everything you want to do when you are a child of God. God does not what to be first on your priority list. He wants to be the only one on your list. You please Him and He will take care of all else. That's the way He works. It requires trust, but, it also require faith and patience. God might not be there when you think you need Him, but, He is always on time. His schedule is more dependable than yours because He knows some things that you do not know. There are humans who you love, but, do not have faith in and do not trust. They have their weaknesses and their limitations. God does not have these problems. When the road gets rocky, that is when the extent of your love for the Lord will be obvious. That is when you will find out how much you love God. Hardships don't last always. Making it through the storm is important, but, only when you learn to dance in the rain will you know you have arrived. That's what He is good at. Taking care of you when times are hard. Nobody said the road would be easy. But, I don't believe He brought me this far to leave me. I really love the Lord.

SABBATH

We serve a jealous God. Remember the Sabbath and keep it Holy. God made the seventh day of the week the Sabbath. The Holy Day. The day when we are to put everything aside and give Him our attention. By what authority has man changed the Sabbath Day? The seventh day of the week is Saturday. Why do Christians go to church on the first day of the week, Sunday?

Some will state that the Resurrection of Jesus is the reason. Don't believe it. Emperor Constantine in 312 A.D. is one reason. He had no God given authority to change anything God Commanded. Man has taken it upon himself to change the Lord's Day. It makes you wonder how many other changes in has made.

We serve a very understanding God. He wants us to work. He also wants us to take time out of our lives to show Him appreciation for His blessings. One day out of seven is all He has commanded. One day to put aside all other concerns and honor and praise our Creator. Time is one of the most valuable blessing God has given you. You show Him your love and appreciation by giving back to Him a part of this blessing.

He has not told you when He will call your name because He wants you to get ready and stay ready. You have to keep plenty of lamp oil nearby because He might come in the mid of the night. Are you ready?

Honor the Sabbath.

REDEEMER

Sin is always waiting at the door. Waiting for us to slip, trying to get us to deviate from the right and go wrong. Trying to make us less than we should be ought to be. We will be hard pressed to find the word in the four gospels. We seldom us the word. What is the meaning of Redeemer? It means paid in full. When Jesus said while on the Cross, "It is finished", He was telling us that remission for our sins had been paid in full.

Jesus knew the importance of destroying sin. He also had complete knowledge of man. He knew that sin would always be the only part of the nature of man that could keep him from God. He knew that it was up to Him to save man from his sinful nature. Jesus could only accomplish this by giving Himself as a ransom for all mankind. For the wages of sin is death. But the gift of God is eternal life in Christ Jesus our Lord. Where, O death, is your victory, your sting?

We must understand both the meaning and purpose of His sacrifice. We must understand our responsibilities with respect to His sacrifice. We must sincerely and completely repent. Seek God's forgiveness for our sins. We must believe in the goodness of God. He looks beyond our faults to see your needs. Forgiveness of sin is a need. We must change. When we turn toward anything, we turn away from something. We must turn away from the will of Satan and to the Will of God.

Nothing this good can ever be free. Freedom is not free. Many people have and will die for it. Salvation is not free. Don't think for a minute that Jesus did it all, therefore you don't have any responsibilities. Our Redeemer's blood on Calvary has demands. We must understand what it means being a Christian. There is no forgiveness without repentance. There is no Salvation without surrender. There is no life without death. There is no believing without committing. You cannot have the grace of God without the government of God.

I know my Savior lives.

RESPECT

A feeling that someone has value. Learning to respect others starts at an early age. A school yard bully is a person who lacks respect for others. The foundation of a lasting marriage is respect. Slavery is a result of a lack of respect for others. Respect must not always be earned, but, it can be forfeited. We should respect others for no other reason than they are children of God. But, if he or she refuses to live in a Godly manner, that respect can be forfeited.

There are things you will not do when you are a respectable person. It is beneath you. You have more dignity than that. Character is the foundation of self-respect. Character is the combination of qualities or traits that distinguishes an individual.

Most important, we will respect God. We show respect for God by showing respect for His children. Believe it or not, there are some people who have stated that most people don't deserve respect. It is unimaginable that a person such as this could ever become President of the United States. Or is it? Most people have a degree to their self-respect. They will show respect only when you are looking. You are not looking in the voting booth. It is hard to accept, but, most people do not really care how another person acts as long as they are not affected. Real respect for others is not a universal trait. The devil knows this. He will keep working on you until he finds the breaking point. It might be small. A cashier gives you too much change. If might be big. You find a large amount of money that does not belong to you. Once Satan finds that breaking point, you are his.

There is nothing more valuable to an individual than self-respect. You cannot demand that others respect you when you do not respect yourself. People who have God in their lives demands self-respect of themselves because they know that anything less shows disrespect for their God. The love of God will make you do somethings you never thought you could. The love of God will make you into a person you never thought you could be. What an awesome God we serve. When we think of His blessings, we must come to Him with humility. When we think of our God, we know that we must surrender all. We know there is nothing more Important than RESPECT for our Heavenly Father.

SUFFERING

We were not put here to understand God. God has told us that our ways are not His ways. Why does our merciful loving God permit innocent little children to suffer? The bible does not provide an answer. Nobody knows the answer. We come by hard times. We ask the question, what did I do to deserve this? We are to trust in the goodness of our God. All things work for the good for those who love God and are called for His purpose.

We have some insight into suffering. We have learned that suffering is inescapable, indiscriminate, irrespective of character, impersonal, inhumane, impervious to consequences and irrational. Pain/ suffering is also private and personal. Pain is important. Constant pain is often a reminder that something is wrong. It is a warning. Something has to be corrected. There is no way to avoid pain and suffering, therefore, we must use it as an asset to our lives. If you do not control it, it will control you.

We are invited into a lifetime relationship that is based not on understanding but on loving faith. The good thing is that we do not have to deal with pain and suffering alone. We do not have to live this life alone. Surely, I am with you always, to the end of the age. Jesus suffered. It is not for us to wonder why. It is just for us to do the Will of God, then die. I go to prepare a place for you. For where I am there you shall be also.

I AM

I AM that I AM. God has made it clear that He is not to be questioned or tested. He is God all by Himself. We humans cannot stop thinking about this life. We historically and continually place our minds toward the here and now, not the hereafter. We know that this life is nothing more than a temporary assignment. Yet, we continue to follow the same path. We know that there is a force greater than man. We believe that there is a place greater than earth. Yet, heaven can wait. We will not accept the fact that tomorrow was meant for some, but, tomorrow many never come.

God knows there are some situations that we simply cannot handle. He does not trust us with all things for this reason. God plans to keep you in your place. Your place is to serve and worship Him not to understand Him. If you were in charge, things would be like heaven. Then where would be the fruits of heaven? Life is a test. The difference is that you cannot steal the answers. You pass the test by giving your life to the Glory of God. By putting your faith in things eternal. By accepting the fact that there is nothing on this earth more important than your trust in God. By understanding that God controls whatever He wants to control. God has a purpose. We do not fully understand it all, but, we believe He has a purpose.

I AM simply means that He is present. Even you can honestly say this. That I AM means no one and nothing contributed to His being. He is the beginning and the end. Alpha and Omega. He started it all and He will end it all. Nothing is present on the face of this earth without His permission. That includes you. Nothing will remain on the face of the earth without His permission. That includes you. Give it up. Either you will accept Him as the Center of your life, or, you will not. It is just that simple. That's one source you never what to hear say (you are fired). If your boss would say it, you can find another job. When God speaks those words, you will be in trouble.

Give God the Glory.

BLESSINGS

How can there be good without also bad? Can you believe that a person has been blessed, bestowed happiness and prosperity upon, without reasoning that another has been cursed, damned? Does the word blessing really apply to human beings or should it only be used to honor, exalt, and glorify God and Jesus?

How can one know the meaning of good without also knowing the meaning of bad to compare? Accepting that which happens in this world without understanding goes against human nature. Accepting the death of a child, too young to have sinned, without reason is difficult. This life cannot be heavenly because human beings are not heavenly. All humans will never be heavenly. The word blessing, as is the word suffering, is not to be understood by man. This is the way God wants it.

You have been placed here to get ready for heaven. The reward for your love of God is greater than you can imagine. No one said this road would be easy. You must fight a good fight, stay the course, and keep the faith. Faith that your God will lead you to the Promised Land. Faith that this will be your ultimate blessing.

WHY?

Why was it so important to Jesus that all people believe that He is the Son of God? Why give those who would not believe more reason to kill Him? The primary charge against Jesus was the statement that He is the Son of the Blessed One. Yes, the enemies of Jesus would have come up with other charges to accomplish their objective to kill Jesus, but, none as profound as "I AM".

There is no greater love than to give one's life for another. Only by making it known that God was willing to lay down the life of His Son could it be made evident that God so loved the world. Because Jesus lives, we live. There is a judge for the ones who reject Him and will not accept His word. They will all be condemned on the last day.

The only way God could get His message through to us was to physically come to earth and become, in body, one of us. God knew that there would be many non-believers, therefore, He gave Jesus many heavenly powers. Powers unlike any human being. They hated Him so much that they refused to believe in anything He did. Why? They had their own concept as to what the Christ would look and be like. They had their own believes as to the reason their Christ would come to earth. Jesus did not come to save them from Roman oppression. He came to Save their Souls. The Souls of all who loved God and would show their love by accepting Him as the Son of God.

The work of God is this, to believe in the One He has sent.

DEEP WITHIN

We all have problems many of which we bring on ourselves. Some of our problems are caused by others. Life presents enough problems without dealing with those caused by others. This world is full of people who need help. There is only one kind of help that can be an assist to all. Spiritual help. We must take control of our problems or they will control us. We must pray for wisdom and the understanding that other people cause us problems because they are in need of help.

Dealing with our problems and the problems of others will always be a part of our lives. Jesus knew that He would not be able to cure all people from physical illness. That is the reason He never addressed the issue of suffering. Jesus gave us a means to control and manage our problems. That means is the Holy Spirit. Believe it or not, the Holy Spirit is even more available than Jesus because the Holy Spirit can be in many different places at the same time. It permits us to work our way through any situation recognizing that we live in an imperfect world and that we are imperfect people trying to serve a perfect God. There are no problems in life beyond our control because the Holy Spirit is deep within. For nothing can be out of control when God is in control.

JOY

We have a bad habit of thinking God works on our time schedule. We too often expect joy to find us. We will not trip over it. We can show God appreciation for this day or we can go about business taking His gift for granted. With age comes wisdom if we accept it. Too many young people leave this world without ever discovering the true gift of God.

I know why the caged bird sings. True joy comes from deep within. Too often we look for joy in all the wrong places. We find joy in our love for the Lord and for others. Often times we make the statement, I know how you feel. You could only know how that person feels when you have walked in that person's shoes. The joy of giving is realized when we give of ourselves. Only when we give the most precious gift of all, our time, are we truly blessed.

Giving of your time to bring joy to another person is a blessing. You can help to bring joy into the life of another by giving yourself. You are the greatest gift of all. Let the Holy Spirit work through you by releasing God's Spirit to others. I know why the caged bird sings. The Spirit of God.

TALK

You talk too much. If you can't find something good to say about a person, don't say anything at all. The person you are talking about is a child of God. Oh, it will never get back to him/her. Then why say it? If it will not make for a positive change, why say it? Even constructive criticism can be damaging if that person you are talking to is not ready to receive it in good spirit. Wise men store up knowledge and understanding, but, the mouth of a fool invites ruin.

How much better it would be to make it our goal to say only that which is positive. Mature believers have advanced to the stage of never becoming a stumbling block to others. We often hear people say, I am going to say it anyway because it is the truth. Words are dynamite. Words can destroy people. We should be very careful before we do anything that we cannot undo. Once said, you cannot take it back even if you had good intentions when saying it.

Not being right, but, love builds people up. We should never cause a child of God to fall into sin. We should never say anything that makes it more difficult for another to draw closer to God. We have the liberty to say almost anything. Take heed lest by any means this liberty becomes a stumbling block to another.

YOUR BODY

Glorify God with your body. Sin always lies at the door. Waiting for you to deviate from the right way and go wrong. Trying to get you to fail to be what you ought to be, could be, should be. We live in a permissive society. The church should always stay in tune with the Will of God. When the church lets God down, we can only depend upon our personal connection with God to direct us. Scripture tells us that all things are expedient and we should not be brought under the power of any. Fighting sin takes commitment and effort. Your body is a gift from God. It has been paid for at a very high price. You are no longer your own. Your body is not yours to do as you please. Scripture tells us that our bodies are members of Christ. You have no right to mistreat the property of God.

Stop playing games with God. God hates sin. Anything that excites disgust. Detestable acts or practices. Deliverance demands holiness. There are dangers in submitting to temptation. We must realize that Victory over temptation must be a calculated decision. Relying on emotions alone is a dangerous and unreliable route. It will not accomplish Victory. Our goal is Victory in Jesus.

FRIENDSHIP

Relationship. It is possible to be a relative yet not have a relationship. It could be out of your control. That person is your relative and you could not change it even if you wanted to. A friendship is a very special relationship simply because it is by choice, within our control. The word love is used without restriction to a family member, but, not toward friends. A man will seldom tell a male friend, I love you. Yet, a close true friend is a rare bond of love. The word thanks, used more with friends than family. We must think that an immediate family member has an obligation, but, a friend does not.

Because no one is forced into the relationship of a friend, no one is forced into the degree of a relationship. A person can be your friend without being committed to make sacrifices. Finding that person who is willing to suffer without return is rare. We seem to show more appreciation to a close friend than a family member. The perfect friendship is a person who does not force themselves on you. A person who is honest and up front. A person you can go to anytime of the day or night for help. Who you don't have to worry about over hauling with your problems. A person you can learn from who will help you live a better life. A friend who will let you know that you would be wise to put your trust in things eternal. A person who has promised to be with you always even until the end of the age.

Oh, want a friend we have in Jesus. We can look the world over and we will never find another like Him. He has made life so easy. All we have to do is accept and obey Him. You must prove your love for Him if your destination is heaven. Proof comes in the why you live. God will hold you accountable for the way you live your life. Each one will receive what is due him for the things done while in the body whether good or bad. Friendship is a choice. I'm so glad that long ago I made Jesus my choice.

STATUS

Christians have status. Their status might be guess, visitor, fan, or servant. The primary purpose of the church is to bring people to God. People who go to church have different status. A guess is one who shows up now and then. A visitor is one who shows up with regularity on Sunday only. It does not manner if you are a member. You are a visitor if the work of God is only a once a week practice. Maybe you are a fan of Jesus. An enthusiastic admirer of Jesus Christ. You think you are saying all the right things so Jesus should be more than satisfied. Some will not accept the fact that as Christians our work validate our faith. Service is a word most of us try to avoid. When we read through the four gospels telling of the life of Jesus, we will find that Jesus said believe in me about five times. He said follow me about twenty-five times.

Jesus is not looking for cheerleaders, fans who sit in the stands or pews and cheer Him on. We as Christians have to work for the betterment of God's Kingdom. We cannot be more involved in things that will be, sooner or later, taken from us anyway. Freedom is not free. People have died for it. Salvation is not free. It will cost you something to follow Jesus. Read the fine print. If anyone would come after me, he must deny himself and take up the Cross (daily) and follow Me. There is no comfortable way to carry that Cross. It is heavy and awkward. A symbol of humiliation. People have died trying to carry it. God's ultimate goal for your life is not comfort. His goal for you is Christ like character if you are going to be a follower of Jesus Christ. There is no forgiveness without repentance. There is no Salvation without complete surrender. There is no life without death. There is no believing without committing your life to God.

AGAINST ALL ODDS

There are some people who play the odds. Why not believe? The rewards are great, if you are right, and cost you nothing if you are wrong. They are not fooling God. God knows your heart. He will test you to see if your heart controls your actions. It is necessary to prove that which you confess with your mouth. Or is it? Jesus told the criminal who died next to Him, today you will be with me in paradise. The heart of the criminal was right at his time of death. Does this tell us that if your heart is sincere at death, God will forgive all else? That is another question that remains a mystery. We believe because we want to believe. We want there to be a God. We want Him to be the Creator of all. We want there to be a heaven waiting for us. We don't have to understand it all. Just let it be.

Cover all the bases. Don't be concerned about the odds. Confess with your mouth and believe in your heart. We cannot prove the existence of God because He wants it that way. He does not want you to prove it. He wants you to believe it against all odds. That is the most important part of life. You must answer the first question correctly or everything thereafter will be wrong. You cannot prove that there is a God. That tells us how strong belief really is. Nothing can have an effect on our belief in God. Not even all the reasoning in this world. There are some smart people in this world who can put together a good case disclaiming the non existence of God. We Christians will leave it to the smart ones to question that which we believe. All we want to do is love Him. Nothing will separate us from our Lord.

YOUR HEART

To whom much is given, much is expected. We pray for a pure heart so we can serve Him. Many people who go to church are sincere, however, there are some who will not make the smallest sacrifice if it depended solely on them. They are like a man who looks at himself in a mirror then goes away and immediately forgets what he looks like. There are many people with good hearts who will never make it to heaven. We cannot take the second step until we have taken the first. We must first confess with our mouths that Jesus Christ is Lord. We then must believe in our hearts in His Resurrection. The third and all steps thereafter are absolutely necessary. We are saved by faith alone, but, if faith is alone it is not faith. The body without the Spirit is dead and so faith without deeds is also dead. Jesus made it perfectly clear that we shall all appear before the judgment seat of Christ, that each one may receive what is due him for the things done while in the body.

God will hold you accountable for both the things you do and the things you do not do in this life. A person is justified by what he does and not by faith alone. Talk is cheap. Actions speak louder than words. It is when you give of yourself that you truly give. Listen, God is speaking to you. Feed my sheep. Man cannot live by bread alone, but, by the words of Christ Jesus. For he who would accept His words will hunger no more.

TIME

Our days are numbered. What we do know is that we have this moment to seek God and His wisdom. It takes time and effort to learn about God. We must learn of His love, glory, majesty, power, and authority. Knowledge without love is fruitless. It is better to believe than to have all the facts straight. We must be very careful about what we believe in. We cannot believe everything we hear or read. It takes time and wisdom. Wisdom comes from the Holy Ghost. When we are willing to accept the Holy Spirit in to our lives, we gain an experience that we cannot receive in any other manner. The Holy Spirit is powerful. There are people who cannot read at all who are filled with the Holy Spirit. Only your acceptance of God can permit the Holy Spirit to grow within you. Upon the departure of Jesus, the Holy Spirit empowered His disciples to perform feats that only Jesus could previously accomplish.

There is nothing too hard for God. He has been known for being the God of the least of these. Once you accept Jesus Christ, there will be nothing that you cannot accomplish. Danger will continue to follow you, but, your Protector will be forever present. You will be able to accept whatever life throws at you and handle it. You will stay relaxed in time of storm. You will understand your purpose in life because you will understand that God loves you. God will become the Center of your life, the Center of your Joy. You will feel like you have been born again. There are two births and one life. The most important being when you accept the Father, Son, and Holy Ghost.

VERSIONS

The bible has extraordinary value. Through Jesus Christ, the bible helps us to realize the glory, majesty, power and authority of God. Writers of the bible were inspired by God. They were believers, imperfect as all human beings are, but believed deeply in God and Jesus Christ as the Savior of man.

There were hundreds of Books of written scripture. Catholic Christian leaders made the decision that seventy-three promoted the Christian faith. Protestant leaders decided that only 66 were exactly as they believed. The purpose of the bible was to promote Christianity. Leaders did not want readers to make the decision as to what they believed. Christian leaders printed only what they believed and wanted others to believe.

The bible has been translated from Hebrew, Greek, and Arabic into hundreds of languages by people who, like us, had theological bias. There are over fifty English versions of the bible. They range from that which attempts to be word perfect such as the King James and the New American Standard versions to The Living Bible and Message translated for the purpose of delivering a message at the other end of the equivalence spectrum. The King James version was first placed in the Catholic church by force. The Roman Catholic church did not want people to have bibles because they believed people would stop respecting their position and stop bringing their monies to church.

Since the publication of the King James version in 1611, the English language has changed more than any other language in the world. Scripture has been translated hundreds of times. The writings could not be word perfect. We Christians should cherish the bible. The more we realize about Christ, the more we love God. The better Christians we become, the better human beings we develop into. Jesus is the only way to the Father. He told us, I am the way and the light. No one comes to the Father but through me. I believe ever word Jesus said. Jesus is the only way to our Heavenly Father. The one thing that all the different versions have in common is God, Jesus, and Holy Ghost. Some versions attempt to be word perfect. Others attempt to give the reader more understanding. The better we understand scripture, the more we love God.

MISTAKE

One commits a mistake only when that person thinks they are doing right, but, finds that their actions were wrong. A person who knows the act is wrong before committing it yet does it anyway has not made a mistake. It was an intentional wrongful act that cannot be lessened by placing the word mistake in front of it. Many people offer an apology for wrong doings then call it a mistake. They are simply trying to lessen the action instead of taking full responsibility for that which they have done.

The Sadducees and Pharisees did not make a mistake. They were both ignorant and bias. Jesus called them hypocrites because they gave the impression on the outside that all was clean while on the inside they were condemning themselves to sin. What was more dramatic was that they were blind guides causing others to sin with them.

When we look at many Jewish leaders of today, we find the same characteristics. Jewish leaders still will not accept the God given powers of Jesus. Many Jews are still looking for one who will reign as King, return them to their homeland, and rebuild the Temple. They are looking for a Messianic age of peace and a time in which the knowledge of God fills the earth. God sent Jesus with the primary purpose of saving our Souls not fulfilling Messianic tasks.

No, the Messiah did not come riding a white horse or with the intention of giving Jews heaven on earth. He came to deliver the message of God's love. Blessed are the meek, for they will inherit the earth. Blessed are those who hunger for God's word for they will be filled. Blessed are the pure in heart, for they shall see God.

DADDY-O

Anyone who remembers the greeting daddy-o has to be old. Things have changed from those days. There are a lot of people who simply don't care about others. At what stage in life did you come to the realization that you would not live forever? At what stage did you come to realize that this world is full of bad people that you better stay away from? They were not born that way. What happen?

Knowing why you are here and why you must leave here is not simple for some people. Knowing that all the money in the world will not keep you here is a difficult realization for some. Jesus came here to fulfill the cup given to Him by God. We can only fulfill that cup by dying as did Jesus. We have been told that death was defeated by the Resurrection of Christ Jesus. We must give up these perishable bodies and take on the form of our imperishable spiritual bodies. Our likeness to God.

We have been permitted life for the purpose of honor, praise and worship of our God. He gave us these perishable bodies so that one day He could take them back for the purpose of giving us new life. A life of endless duration where we will forever give Him praise.

DO THE RIGHT THING

It's the truth and I'm going to tell it because it's the right thing to do. Are you saying it because it is the right thing or are you saying it because you want to help make for a change for the better? How many times have you heard a person say (that's scripture)? They are actually saying, that is my interpretation of scripture. Look at the Ten Commandments. It states the Lord will punish children for the sins of their fathers to the third and fourth generations. It does not state that children will be punished for all sins that are committed by their fathers. Scripture tells us that each person must answer for his own actions, good and bad. Not the sins of others. God is telling us that if generation after generation continue to worship a god before Him, He will not be pleased. Scripture must be taken in content. Without content considerations, it is impossible to be sure of the correct meaning of scripture. Without the correct meaning, you cannot be sure that you are doing the right thing.

The primary reason we should offer our input where there is a situation of stress is to help make things better, not because we feel that we are correct and that we are doing the right thing. When we say things, even when we are right, that we know will not make things better we are not doing the right thing. We should never become a stumbling block to others. We can become a stumbling block even when we are right. Having the wisdom to know when to speak and how to say it can come only from the Holy Spirit. A person who can put up with difficult people, resisting the temptation to retaliate, ignore, or make statements that do not improve the situation has received wisdom from the Holy Ghost. Knowledge without love is fruitless. True love always wants what is best for other people. The understanding of God's way enables us to do the right thing as children of God.

INTERPRETATION

How many different meanings can you think of for the word trunk? A single word can have many completely different meanings. The Old Testament was written primarily in Hebrew with some Aramaic and then translated into Greek. The New Testament was written in Greek which was the legal language during these times of the Roman Empire. Therefore, the Old Testament was translated from Hebrew and Aramaic to Greek to English making for the possibilities for numerous human errors. Each book is also colored by the historical settings in which it was written. The political, social, philosophical, and religious conditions of the times came to bear on what was expressed distorting and detracting from the word of God. For these reasons, anyone who tells you that the version of the bible you are reading is the exact words as written by the original writers are simply not using good reasoning.

Translation is extremely important to determine correct interpretation and correct interpretation is extremely important in determining correct understanding. The bible was formulated to promote Christianity. The only writings permitted to be a part of the bible where the writings that agreed completely with the believes of those people on the selection committee. It is with faith. Men like Stephen were martyrs far before the bible was published. Christians today have a publication that can help in our better understand of the love of God. The bible is for those who have already been touched by the Holy Spirit.

Understanding God's word takes time, effort and a keen sense of observation. What does the passage say, mean, and how does the meaning apply to me? Context is extremely important. That which surrounds or goes with the text. Without proper context, correct meaning can be completely lost. True study of scripture focuses on detail. There are many study helps to assist us in understanding. Subject guides and bible concordance help in the interpretation of meaning as related to the original language word from which the English language word was translated. There are also Hebrew and Greek dictionaries as well as Greek study books.

It is time to become more than just a reader of God's word. It's time to better understand God's purpose for your life.

BORN AGAIN

We cannot earn Salvation, but, we can lose it by the way we live. A good person lives in a manner that can be conceived as acceptable to God. A person who would do anything he/she could to help another, but, has not accepted God as Creator and Jesus as Savior. Will this person be saved? There are many who have knowledge gathered through formal education. They might be theologians or might have graduated from a seminary. Yet, they can only offer their opinion. They can reason, but, they cannot prove a thing. It seems we do not have enough appreciation for the term Divine Revelation. From what seminary did Jesus graduate? There are some who have knowledge through education, but who are lacking in love. The Pharisees were very knowledgeable in religion, but, lacking in love. Every mature believer having knowledge that others do not have must also receive divine revelation from God to be successful. Only through divine revelation will we receive insight into the mysteries of the Holy Spirit formerly hidden but not revealed in the gospel of God.

Jesus tells us that except a man be born again, he cannot see the kingdom of God. Your education, knowledge, ancestors, descendants, position in the church, religious convictions and habits do not matter. It is about our background that He is telling us that we must be born again. Our birth into this world is not our Salvation.

We are not born saved. We are born sinners. Man is a creature of two elements, physical and spiritual. Adam disobeyed God. At that moment, he died spiritually and began to die physically. Only by accepting God and Christ Jesus into your life can you be born again. The person on the inside will come out. You can feel His presence within you. You know deep within when you no longer belong to yourself.

You belong to God.

FOUNDATION

The lost generation. Drugs use to be considered dangerous to one's health. Now grass is legal in many States. When did it all change? The changed started when man stopped being head-of-household. We lost it when man decided that it was not his responsibility to raise his children. When males decided that a better house or car was more important than their relationship with their son or daughter. When the father started making statement like, my child never saw the inside of a daycare center. Their mother was always there for them because I worked long hours to support the whole family. Would it have been wiser to have done with less materially and given more of yourself to your family?

Raising children is the primary responsibility of the father, not the mother. The father is the head-of-household. Every family needs two pastors. One at church and one at home. The family that goes to church together, prays together, has dinner together, stays together. There is no substitute for a full-time father. Children love but do not listen to Mom the way they listen to Dad. We lost it when God stopped being head of our households. For no one can lay any foundation other than the one laid, which is Jesus Christ. Train a child in the way he should go, and when he is old he will not turn from it. Parents who do not discipline their children are in danger of ruining them.

Foundation. We need to get back to the basics. The word of God. A strong family can only be realized through the leadership of a strong father and our Heavenly Father.

DISCIPLINE

God made your butt one of the softest parts of your body for two reasons. You sit on it so much and because your mom or dad is going to strike it if you don't act right. How many children have you heard of being admitted to the hospital because of a sore butt? Of course, that child psychologist you have been listening to, who has no children, knows more than God.

Scripture tells us, do not withhold discipline from a child. If you punish him with the rod, he will not die. Punishment is a form of love. An adult might say no simply because it is morally wrong. A child will get away with as much as an adult permit. One reason you will not do certain things is because you fear the consequences. Fear can be a good thing. As you grow older, you come to understand that the words fear and respect have a lot in common. Fear of the Lord is the (beginning) of wisdom.

We must learn the consequences of wrong doing. We can wait until that child spends some time in jail to find that out. You can visit him on weekends. Discipline is a lesson Christians must also learn. The Lord will forgive you if you sincerely repent, however, that does not mean that He will not discipline you for your wrong actions. The Lord will discipline those He loves and punish all He accepts as His children. No discipline seems pleasant at the time, but, painful later on.

We accept the fact that we cannot have the Grace of God without the government of God. The Lord cares enough about us to keep us on the right path of life. He does this through encouragement, teaching, and discipline. The government of God demands discipline.

AMERICA and CHRISTIANITY

What did the founders of this country really want it to be? In 1776, all but approximately 2,500 Jews identified themselves as Christians. Some were not sincere. Some said they were Christians because society would accept them. They called them orthodox Christians because they were influenced by factors other than religion. But then, if man were angels, there would be no need for government.

Each State had the right to establish their own laws with respect to religion. Often times waging taxes on non-Christians and/or non-State churches. There was no National church. Many were slave owners. They stated in the Declaration of Independence that all men are created equal. Did they really mean ALL?

They stated that all man where endowed by the Creator. They were not Deists. They did believe in a clear separation of church and State. This is the reason the separation of church and State is stated in the very First Amendment. All should have the freedom to worship God or not worship God. Founders of this country encouraged Christianity, but, did not mandate it. The Constitution is godless.

The Unite States is a Christian Nation. They did not always practice what they preached with respect to personal liberty. They too were products of their times. No person who states that he is not a Christian has ever been elected President. On currency it is written, in God we trust. When the President is sworn in, He must place his hand on the bible. The birth and Resurrection of Jesus are National Holidays.

Great powers like Egypt, Babylon and Rome have come and gone. None of them had God as it's foundation. It has been difficult. Nobody said the road would be easy. If God is for you, who can be against you. God will not leave America as long as America does not leave God.

WOMEN IN CHRIST

God permitted Jesus to be born of a woman without the involvement of a man. God permitted a woman to be the first to see that Jesus had risen. Yet women continue to play a supporting role in the church of God. Catholic churches will not ordain women into the priesthood. Canon Law permits the priesthood to be exclusively male. The Southern Baptist Convention has recognized the ordination of women as have Lutheran and United Methodist churches. Women with Baptist organizations have been a continuing debate.

Slavery was a part of the culture when Jesus walked this earth. Culture and climate has had an effect on all writings and human actions. We want scripture to be easy to understand. God gave us minds to think. Many believers do not want to do this, think. There are those who refuse to face the reality that man has infected the written word. Men much more so than women.

There are a great number of people who need to hear the Word of God. We should not permit a hermeneutical problem to prevent this connection. A clean heart, not gender, should be the chief human characteristic to determine church leadership. Saving Souls regardless of how or by whom. Jews, Gentiles, Protestants, Catholics, males, females all are needed in the effort to bring people to God.

HARVEST

The farmer plants his seeds on fertile ground. He knows there will be a harvest. He must have patience, wait, and endure. Christians must be fertile and patient while God does His work. It is not necessary to know why only to believe that it is the work of the Lord. By nature, man is not patient. Man wants control. It goes against his nature to give it all to God and wait. Even the patience of God has limits. God has told us to not pray for certain people who have been given every opportunity to change, but, who continue to live a life of wickedness. Sin is contagious. Holiness is not contagious. Even a holy person who stays around a sinful person too long will become less than holy. God told His people to not marry certain people because these people would separate them from their God. We can lean many things of valuable when we read between the lines and think. Not just read words.

Scripture tells us that evil people will be numerous at the time of the return of Jesus. Christians can only spread the Good News to those who will listen. Those who understand their responsibilities and duties in serving God. Those who are willing to be like fertile soil in accepting the word and love of God and are willing to wait on the Lord and the time of harvest. Learning to be more and more like Jesus takes time. Sometimes it takes solitary confinement with Jesus.

God does not function within our instant world. He might not answer when you call, but, God is always on time.

IF THE TRUTH BE TOLD

Jesus is the only One who knows more about you than you know about yourself. Only God knows what is truly in your heart. Jesus came to clean up our mess. We made this mess because we would not follow the Commandments of God. We today have the word of God. We have no excuses. We know what God wants of us. The knowledge that Jesus brings us makes it much easier to determine God's truth. Jesus knew what was in Peter's heart. Jesus told Mary Magdalene to tell His disciples and Peter that He has risen. Why, "… and Peter"? Jesus wanted Peter to know that He would always love him. Jesus knows our weaknesses. If the truth be told, we shall never be separated from the love of God. We might deny Him in many different ways, but, never in our hearts. God will never give us up. God will never give up on anyone of His children who have a clean heart. The power of God's love can overcome our weaknesses.

Pray for a clean heart. Pray that God will give you a clean heart so you can serve Him. Pray that He will fix your heart so that you may be use by Him. Pray that you will be blessed so much that your life will be a blessing to the world in the name of Jesus. Ask and it shall be given. Seek and you will find. Knock and the door will be open unto you. God will come into your heart, if you will only ask.

SIN

The enemy of mankind. We are born sinners. We are not sinners because we sin. We sin because we are sinners. Sin will destroy one who does nothing to stop it. Sin is always at the door waiting for us to slip so that he can prevent us from being what we could be, ought to be, should be. We must each find Jesus for ourselves. Think of the many who have grown up in strong Christian families who have still gone wrong. Holiness is not contagious. Regardless of your holiness, you will lose your religious ways if you hang around the wrong people long enough. There are some people even Jesus could not save. We serve a God of grace and mercy, but, you can push Him too far. Those who think they can take advantage of the goodness of God will find out the hard way that God don't play that.

You might go to church almost every Sunday. You still might not make it to heaven. It takes a lot more than being a one day a week Christian. If you make it to heaven, the only person you should be surprise to see is yourself. What is she doing here? God did not ask you to do His job. You don't have the qualifications. He is God all by Himself. He gave you your assignment. That is your responsibility. God does not take away from you to give to another if you are faithful to Him. He has made a number of promises to you. God has never broken a promise.

The parable of the father who showed love and generosity to his son who returned home after going astray has a message for us. We have to stop thinking like the older brother. The generosity of the father to the younger son had no negative affect on the older brother. We should enjoy it when God blesses others and hope that such blessings will be a benefit to many. When we give thanks to God for blessing others, we find that our blessings increase.

Thinking, acting, reasoning, and loving like Jesus is our mission. The armor of Jesus protects us from sin. Nothing can be out of control when God is in control. Sin is helpless when God is in control of your life. If more people only understood this, it would be like taking food out of the Devil's mouth. He would starve to death. Or, go back where he belongs. Hades.

I SHOOKUP THE WORLD

When we hear this phrase, we often think of the greatest boxer of all times. He was a fighter outside as well as inside the ring. There is One who shook up the world even more. Because of Him, there are over two billion Christians on the face of the earth and counting. The largest faith in the history of mankind.

He never lost a fight. He never broke a promise. His right cross is God. His left hook is love. He didn't stay here long, but, He stayed long enough to shakeup this world. He let us know of the love of God. He let us know by example of the sacrifices necessary to please God. We can love no one more than God. We must love God with all our heart, soul, mind, and strength. We must love one another as ourselves. We must not expect rewards here on earth. We must all stand before the judgment seat of Christ to answer for that which we have gone while in the body. The pure in heart shall see God. The rewards for loving God are greater than the human mind can imagine.

We live our lives for the primary purpose of hearing Jesus say, well done My good and faithful servant.

He shook up the world. The Greatest of all times. JESUS.

PRODUCTIVE GROWTH

Why should you continue to take up space and air, yet, not fulfill your purpose? You are going through each day of your life trying to gain more materially. In case you didn't know it, all that you gain will be taken away. You will be back to zero. Is this your purpose for living? Nothing. You might be able to enjoy it for a short time. Maybe. But sooner or later, it will all be gone.

We must understand our purpose for living. Why did God decide that He wanted to give me this life? The answer to that question will define your purpose. Then we must decide how to fulfill our purpose. We were placed here is do a few things very well not to be a trick of all trades. It is important to God and to society to be exceptional in a few things. Some people have a number of letters behind their names. It is better to have the phrase (a child of God) behind your name. All other purposes are secondary to that of accepting God into your life.

God is concerned about not your physical or financial growth, but, your spiritual productive growth. You must have a dream. If you do not have a dream, how are you going to have a dream come true? Your productive growth is that which Jesus died for. Growth in the Spirit of God. When you find that you are falling short, like the fig tree, maybe you need to loosen the soil around your roots and add a little fertilizer. Break some of those bad habits and create new good habits. Get some people out of your life and include some people who will help you in your efforts to grow productively.

You owe it to Jesus. He suffered greatly to give you the opportunity to grow productively. We owe it to God. He put us here not to just exist, take up space, inhale His air. He wants us to grow productively in His Spirit. That is the one thing that dying cannot take away from us. This joy I have. This world didn't give it and this world can't take it away. When you die, the real you and the joy that is within your heart and soul will be beamed up to your everlasting life with your Maker for eternity.

WHO DO YOU TRUST

There are numerous Christian preachers and writers all of whom do not deliver the same message. The bible is full of miracles. We must believe in miracles if we are to believe in the bible. A miracle is that which can only be attributed to a supernatural or Divine source. Jesus is a miracle. A Divine Marvel who was perfect in every way. When making the decision as to trust, we must first make the decision as to WHO to trust.

Every human who has ever lived has made mistakes and made incorrect statements. They might have tried to get it right. They might have had great faith, but, they were human. Sometimes we do not have the wisdom to determine where those mistakes might be. It was not meant to be black and white. Christianity makes it necessary to consider all available then make a decision. You could be right or wrong. You will never find out while in this world. Your decision is based on trust.

Christians have decided to place their trust in Jesus. Numerous bibles print the words of Jesus in Red. Words of all others are subject to mistake. Those who composed the bible published only what they believed. That does not mean that it is not true.

Trust in God, Christ Jesus, and the Holy Ghost. Only these three are perfect.

SOMEBODY IS WATCHING YOU

Christianity is on the decline. Christians are dying faster than others are accepting Christianity. Church membership is decreasing. Maybe there is a need for something to drive people to God. People can think. They know that this life is not forever. Most people follow. Being popular means doing what the crowd is doing. Jesus told us not to conform to this world. Popularity was not one of the goals of Jesus. He knew what was right and nothing would keep Him doing that which was right.

As Christians, we are both leaders and followers. It is our job to lead others to God by following the teachings of Jesus. Hitting people over the head with the bible will not get it done. Turning the state of Christianity around in the United States will be a slow process. It will be done by Christians who know their responsibilities and live life as if somebody is watching them. Jesus is not the only one watching you. That person next door. That minor who you are not paying attention to. The way you live your life makes an impression on others. That is one reason God wants you to obey His Commandments. Not only for your personal benefit, but, also for the benefit of others. That is the reason Jesus was so hard on the Pharisees. Jesus called them hypocrites and said, "You shut the kingdom of heaven in men's faces. You yourselves do not enter, nor will you let those enter who are trying to".

As a Christian, we have a responsibility to live like somebody is watching. To live like God would have us live. That is one way that we spread the Good News. I am a Christian, a child of God. Watch me. I want you to watch me because God is with me and He will be with you. You might think that nothing bothers me. You might think that I work so hard and don't seem to mind it. I'm just like you. I have just as many problems as you have. I have learned not to tell my God how big my problems are. I have learned to tell my problems how big my God is. I have learned to dance in the rain because I know trouble don't last always. My future is not as much here as there. All I have to do is endure. My God has already taken care of the rest. All of this will end, but, my love for God will last forever. I'm going to make the best of things while I am here, but, it makes me feel so good believing that the best is yet to come. Look at me. I'm as happy as a human being can be. And I feel like I'm clinging to a cloud. I can understand, it is Jesus holding my hand.

Somebody is watching. I'm so glad someone is watching.

PURPOSE

When you were a teen or in your twenties, you believed the world was made for you. You were on the fast track. When you were in your thirties and forties, work and family were your priorities. When you hit fifty and sixty, you started to realize that this life was more than half over. You accepted the fact that all the knowledge, feelings, and wisdom that you have will leave here with you. The years are passing so fast. Why am I here?

You start giving God some attention. You develop the understanding that there is no forgiveness without repentance, no Salvation without complete surrender, no life without death, and no believing without commenting. Your start to think back over your life and realized that you did not do it alone. What now? What should you do with all of this faith, wisdom, knowledge, and feelings while you are here? We should realize that throughout the ages, God has raised up ordinary people like you and me, and used them to accomplish great works for His kingdom.

If we do not share, it will be forever lost. Anyone who knows the good he ought to do and does not do it, sins. It happens by doing over and over again until it becomes a habit. Our purpose is to do the work of God. This is the reason He put us here. He will not wait forever for you to respond. What is your life? You are like a mist that appears for a moment then vanishes. It is the Lord's Will for us to live and do His Will.

LIFE'S BIG QUESTION

Why did God permit you a limited number of years on this earth? Could it be that He has given you limited time to decide your answer to life's big question. Overcoming the temptations of life is difficult. Temptation is the strongest element standing between you and God. Trouble is a part of life. Much of the time, you cannot avoid it. It is a test of your faith. God's role is to help you fight temptation and to help you through the stages of trouble. You will receive His help only if you believe in Him. Believing in Him is more than just saying you do. Faith requires patience. Faith requires an understanding that it is not going to happen when you want it to happen and it might not even happen the way you think it will. Faith also requires the understanding that just because you want it does not mean that God wants it. Father, Your Will be done.

Words like temptation and fear are not always bad. You could be tempted to do something good. When we know what God expects of us, good temptations will override bad. Once we give the problem to God don't worry, pray. If you are going to worry, don't pray. If you are going to pray, don't worry. Trust in the goodness of the Lord and in His love for you. Trust that He will make the decision that is best for you.

Reading the Sermon of the Mount can lead you to think that it is impossible to please God. No human being can live up to those standards. One cannot understand the Sermon on the Mount without grasping its eschatological orientation. The branch of theology that treats death, judgment, and the future state of the Soul. You are not perfect. You are not Jesus. Be all that you can be. Be the best most faithful Christian you can be. Let the Spirit control. The rest is in the hands of Christ Jesus.

YOU CAN'T HELP EVERYONE

If people do not welcome you, shake the dust off your feet when you leave their town. That is what Jesus told His disciples. Jesus wants everyone to be given the opportunity to believe and accept His gospel. Not all will. It is our responsibility to spread the Good News. It is the job of the Holy Spirit to move within a person and bring that person to God.

There are some people that Jesus could not help. It is hard to accept, but, some people are beyond help. Too many people are more interested in their welfare in this life than their eternal welfare. Then there are bullies. Forcing another person into an act, any act. God does not believe in force. Forcing a people into any action is a sin. You cannot have a good relationship with everyone. To be honest, there are some people it would be best to stay away from. We as Christians must also understand that we will be rejected more times than accepted. We must stay on the battlefield for our Lord. Our shooting percentage might be low, but, every time we score, it is a game winner. A life winner.

TRAIN A CHILD IN THE WAY HE SHOULD GO

David had numerous brothers. Jesse, David's father, had him attending sheep. Jesse did not consider David man enough to hang with his brothers. Jesse was not trying to hurt David. Jesse just didn't know any better. Parental mistakes. The knowledge that most parents have in raising a child comes solely from the way they were raised. Good or bad. Limited knowledge in performing one of the most important jobs in life. Every child is different. Their DNA might even be the same, but, the two people are different. Too many parents expect the child to adjust to them instead of adjusting to the needs of the child. Because a boy does not act like his father does not mean he is weak. How can a boy who would fight a giant be considered weak?

Parents have to stop thinking they can do something they have no experience at doing. Proverbs is a good starting place. A new born today is the same as a new born two thousand years ago. A man learns from experience, but, a wise man learns from the experiences of others. If your boy wants to help you cut the grass, find a way to include him. Don't reject his offer. If your son or daughter likes ballet instead of football or baseball, encourage her or him to be the best he or she can be. Don't turn your back because that is not your bag.

The parent is the person who is responsible for making the right decisions for the child. This includes training in the ways of Jesus. Oh, I want to wait until my child has more understanding. The person who is in need of more understanding is you. Baptism of a child is a step in the right direction just as pre-school. Don't think for a minute that the only people the Holy Spirit comes to are people who are in full understanding. When a six-year old child on his sick bed, ask you to pray with him, you know this is true.

You will thank God for the birth of your child by dedicating the life of your child to God through Jesus the Christ. Train a child in the way he/she should go. By telling you this, God has given you the decision- making authority. Train your child in the love of God.

DEPENDING ON GOD'S GRACE

We are not sinners because we sin. We sin because we are sinners. Eve started it. Since then we have been on the defensive fighting sin. God knows your heart, but, there is still question about your sincerity. There are more ways to sin than simply not obeying the Ten Commandments. A person who know right from wrong yet does wrong has committed more of a sin than an ignorant person. Which person do you think is in the better Graces of God, a person who lives life in the right manner, who helps others, but, has never said that Jesus is Lord or a passive Christian who keeps to him/her self and does nothing for others? Jesus came to earth to help people. That tells us what He wants us to do. An, I ain't no trouble Christian is next to useless to Jesus. What you believe is secondary to what you do. Your knowledge and wisdom must be shared to be meaningful. Or, do you simply want to take them to the grave with you?

When helping people becomes a habit, we know that the Holy Spirit is alive and working in us. Stop trying to impress God. Stop trying to get to the other side. God will take you to the other side if you follow His Will and His Ways. We must all depend upon the Grace of God because we are all sinners. It is time to become a refined Christian. One who does God's Will out of love for Him and His children.

SEPARATION

It started a long time ago. Jews saw themselves separate from all other people. If you were not a Jew, you were a Gentile regardless of believes or skin color. Why is there so much religious separation? Baptist, Methodist, Lutheran, Church of God, Southern Baptist Convention, National Baptist Convention, National Baptist Convention of America. If you read the Mission statements of these groups, you would be hard pressed to tell which organization that mission statement belongs to. People coming to America from Scotland and other European areas did not leave their religion at home. This is to be understood. It is American religious separation that is hard to take.

Think of the social and political power that could be generated through unity. 30 million strong could change many decisions and many lives for the better. Leaders of these groups are very much like the Sadducees of Jesus time here on earth. They have more interest in position and control than serving God's people. They are not interested in working together, in unity. That would be too much like right. I don't want to be one of the leaders. I want to be the leader. God is watching.

PRAYER

Scripture tells us our Father in heaven knows our needs before we ask. He is going to do that which He knows is right and necessary regardless of our input. Yet, we are told to pray without ceasing. One of the primary reasons to pray is because Jesus prayed. One of the primary reasons to be baptized is because Jesus was baptized. The Divine One will make the right decisions. God enjoys it when His children pray to Him. Our primary purpose of pray should be praise. When we pray, we connect to God through the Spirit. This permits us a grow closer to God. This permits us to get personal with God. Prayer helps us. Prayer gives us peace of heart and mind. You feel so much better. If you are going to pray, don't worry. If you are going to worry, don't pray. Either you believe in the power and goodness of God or you don't. Nothing is too hard for God. When you pray, instead of tell God how big your troubles are, you need to tell your troubles how big your God is.

Learning how to listen is a big part of learning how to pray. God will speak to you sometimes in a very controlled voice. We must listen closely. God does not want to be your consultant. The one you go to only when you cannot handle it all by yourself. He does not want to be your co-pilot. One who you turn to only when you need a break in life and need help. He does not want to hear from you only when you are in trouble. God wants full custody of your life, not just Sunday visits. Twenty-four seven control of your heart, mind, body, and Spirit.

Praise His Holy Name.

LEAD ME

Some of the things I tell my pillow nobody should. Wisdom generates understanding, insight, a different way of seeing things. Wisdom can only come from God. Short of Jesus and the Holy Spirit, there is no greater gift given to man than wisdom. Sin has a powerful tendency to grow and thoroughly dominate one who does nothing to stop it. We can become so weak that sin not only wins the battle but also wins the individual war. Sin can be controlled. There is one thing that gives sin the devil. Forgiveness. Forgiveness is one of the most difficult blessings for humans to accept. When people hurt us, the hurt is deep. Forgiveness is an excellent measure of growth in the Spirit of God. We so many times ask God for forgiveness, but, we find it so hard to forgive others.

Oh, if we could only live this life over again. There are so many changes, so many decisions, that would be different. Now we are in a trap. We have gotten ourselves in a situation we cannot get out of. We cannot change the past. God's goal is not to punish but to teach. Not to shame but to Save. Each wrong that we bring to Him and confess, He will readily forgive and bring some good out of the aftermath. God does not expect us to be perfect. Perfection is not necessary in order to live a life pleasing in the sight of God. God loves you. He looks beyond your faults and sees your needs. Let God lead you. You will not win every battle, but, Jesus has already won the war. Your reward will be Salvation.

JUNK

God don't make no junk. There are people in this world who have turned into junk. They have no sense of value for the welfare of others. What made them this way? Could it be in their childhood teachings or lack of teachings. We know that children will become that which they are taught to become. Many white children became bigots during slavery only because they were taught to hate. The Only thing we know for sure is that there is no universal answer why people turn into junk. One thing is for sure, that person has given up on himself. They decided to take the easy way out by doing wrong. They have turned into junk because they care only about their physical well-being. That was a major problem with the Israelites. They wanted a savior not a Savior. One who would lead them out of Roman bondage, not one who would save their Souls.

The one thing that is in common with all people who have turned into junk is that they have rejected God. There are many who will not accept Jesus the Christ as their Lord, but, how can anyone not accept the life He lived as an example by which to model their life. We are living in a world of fools stepping on dreams. We so highly value something that we know we will lose anyway. Only a fool would turn God's gift of life into junk. The Lord giveth and the Lord will take away. Blessed be the name of the Lord.

LEADERSHIP

Be careful what you ask for. You might get it. Leadership is demanding. Everyone is a sinner. Nothing would get done without a leader. One cannot lead unless others follow. It takes a lot of wisdom to choose the person whom you will follow. We must be careful who we chose to follow. It could lead us into a lot of hardship. We Christians should not believe everything we hear in church. We must understand that all people are imperfect. Subject to mistakes. The correct choice of a leader does not mean that the road will not be rocky. Christians have endured many heart times in their journey. Jesus was the perfect leader who believed that there was something worth dying for.

We have decided to follow Christ Jesus. Through the leadership of Jesus Christ, more and more people each day are forming a relationship with God. Through the church, we can find Christian leadership. We are so glad that long ago we decided to make Jesus our choice. He promised to be with us always even until the end of the age. Jesus has never broken a promise.

JESUS SAID

There are some bibles that print the words of Jesus in red. It is important to know the words that came out of the mouth of Jesus as distinguished from others. Reading the words of Jesus alone is a book within itself. Jesus had no limitations. He told us that everything spoken by Him was given Him by the Father. I am not alone, but, I and the Father that sent Me. There can be no mistakes in His judgments for He told us He speaks to the world those things which He has heard from the Father. So that those listening could better understand, Jesus give many of His words through parables. The Pharisees and Sadducees were more interested in denying Jesus than hearing the word of God.

Jesus, by His own words, has stated that He is the Resurrection and the life. He that believeth in Jesus, though he were dead, yet shall he live and whosoever live and believeth in Him shall never die. If you will believe, you surely will see the Glory of God. We don't really need to know the words of others. We need Jesus. For if any person serves Jesus, that person honors His Father. From His own mouth, He stated to the Sanhedrin and to Pilate that He is the Son of God. His Crucifixion and His Resurrection would have been less meaningful had it not been clear that Jesus Christ is the Son of God. Blessed be the name of the Lord.

LIFE

What's it all about? Is it just for the moment we live? What is the meaning of life? Why am I here? What is my purpose for living? Is the purpose simply to live and then die? Why is it that some people die young while others last to a very old age? Why is it that some people live happy lives while others face struggle after struggle? Why is it that some hold life so precious while others cause the death of many? Were we meant to be happy or is happiness only a temporary experience?

There is one thing we know about life, it will end. There are more mysteries about life than that which we know. Maybe we hold life so precious because the years are limited. Yet, we do not live life in that manner. We don't treasure each day like it is a precious gift from God. We wake up and we think about everything but God. We care more about being served than serving others.

Our only hope is in God. We will never know the answers to life. We must live each day with God on our minds and in our hearts. We must put our complete faith and trust in Him. Good times will come and go. Trouble don't last always. The love of God is everlasting. It is given freely upon request. Knock and the door will be open. God is life. God is the only reason for life. Everything that we have ever known will leave us with one exception. GOD.

THE WORD OF GOD

Church leaders have a history of making their own decisions rather than following the decisions of God. Many try to separate the Old Testament. They say that since the New Testament, they are not bind by the Old Testament. Are they telling us that they are not bind by the Ten Commandments? Jesus came to enhance, not destroy, the Old Testament.

Satan, Empire Constantine, and the Roman Catholic church are the reasons the Sabbath Day was changed from the 7th day to the 1st day. You will be told that the Resurrection of Jesus was the reason. Church leaders have a way of trying to justify their actions after they have made the wrong decision. No human has the authority to change the Commandment of God.

The Sabbath Day was changed thousands of years before Christ. Babylon practiced sun worship during ancient civilizations. They considered the sun the greatest source of light. They were leaders in astrology. Sun worship – Sunday. The Old Testament tells us that God despised sun worship. This is one reason for the fall of Babylon. After the fall of Babylon, their religious leaders took their habits to Rome. Empire Constantine was in control of the church and State. They adopted sun worship and Christianity. They changed the Sabbath Day and the Roman Catholic church conformed.

There are Christian countries that still respect the word of God by keeping the Sabbath on the 7th day. We would be wise to trust only God, Jesus, and the Holy Ghost. We would be wise to take anything touched by man with a grain of salt.

INSPIRATION

Inspiration comes from God and from people touched by God. Four young men come forward to join the church. They look like any young men you would see on the streets. It is obvious they had discussed this decision and made up their minds before entering the building that Sunday morning. The Spirit of the church hit the ceiling. Inspiration. We cannot make decisions about people solely on what we see. You can't judge a book by the cover. Inspiration can come from the most unexpected sources. We need to stop drawing conclusions about people and start praying for them.

Dreams are a source of inspiration. You must have a dream. If you don't have a dream, how are you going to have a dream come true? It is not enough to simply look up the stairway. We must walk one step at a time. All the way to heaven. God has inspired humans to do great things. One is to write scripture. God inspires, He does not edit. You will make mistakes in your life. We are human. God knows that we are human. That is one reason He give each of us a brain. The ability to determine right from wrong. The ability to examine and gain insight and wisdom. God wants us to use His gifts wisely. If we do not, we are insulting Him. Nothing written by man should not be closely examined. A man might have been inspired by God, but, he was not perfected by God. All men make mistakes. When reading the Word of God, we must understand this, yet, understand that the overall meaning and purpose has not been affected. God is real. Jesus is real. The Holy Ghost is real. Only they are perfect. The primary purpose of the Word of God is inspiration. God has inspired His children to be all they can be. There is nothing more meaningful in your life than being inspired by God.

IT'S NOT ABOUT YOU

When joining any organization, we must accept the fact that decisions must be made that are in the best interest of that body and will help to fulfill the mission of that organization. This includes a church organization. The Covenant of the organization is extremely important. The Covenant states that the majority rules and that anyone not in agreement with the majority should step aside and permit the majority to govern. It means exactly what has been written. No one should have the right to overturn that statement. No one includes the pastor. A pastor who states that a member of the body or board must not only permit the majority to govern, but, also help in the enactment of a decision that he feels is not in the best interest of the church, is in error. That is not what the Covenant states. It's not about you. It is about that which the church has agreed. The Covenant. The Bible.

There are certain things that can be voted on and there are certain things that cannot be voted on. God's Word has already made certain decisions. There is nothing inherently wrong with differences of opinion. There is something wrong with a person who gets the head set in one direction and will not consider another point of view. No one person has all the understanding, insight, and wisdom. A dissent is not necessarily a sign of being contrary or contentious. Sometimes it is better for a person to not stand in the way of a decision that he believe to be wrong than to rock the boat.

When we walk on Holy Ground, we should try to think and be like Jesus. It is not what the Lord will do for you in this life. If He never does another thing for you, you have received more than you deserve. It's not about you. It's about God. It's about Jesus. Father, bless me so much that I will not just be blessed, but, use my life as a blessing to the world in Your name. Stop only thinking about yourself and go out of your way to help others. You are a Christian to praise God and help His people. You don't have to worry, God won't let you down.

GOOD INTENTIONS

We want to do the right thing, but, find out too late that our best wasn't good enough. We might think that the right thing is what is best for the majority of the people. We left out one important factor, God. We become worshippers of mankind, humanists. Our minds and consciences are warped and incapable of thinking and acting correctly and righteously apart from God.

It does not matter what you think. To some degree, it does not matter what you pray for. That does not mean don't pray. Prayer is as much for you as it is for God. God is going to do that which He determines best regardless of what you think or want. You should want it that way. When you think, think about what God wants you to do. God has given you detailed instructions as to what He wants you to do and how He wants you to do it. Don't make the mistakes Moses and King Saul made.

There is someone Supreme to mankind and He has the power to control all. It is difficult for some to believe when they see people suffering all around them. God controls that which He wants to control. He has a plan of action. A way of ruling this world that we are not capable of understanding. Stop trying to figure out God. You don't have the wisdom to do so. This understanding is the greatest understanding of all. He is God all by Himself.

God has made it crystal clear. You know exactly what He approves of and what He does not. There are even some Christian organizations that forget their real purpose. They start thinking more about tradition and building maintenance than about God's people. God has a way of bringing people and organizations in line or putting them out of line.

Regardless of what happens to you, remember to keep God in your everyday living and He will bless you in ways you cannot imagine.

JESUS DIVINE

Much of scripture must be contributed to Divine vision. There is no other way that certain events could have been reported. No one was there to hear the prayer of Jesus at Gethsemane. You have a choice to make. The reporting of man or your belief in the Divine nature of Jesus. Some will tell you that at times the human elements over powered the Divine elements of Jesus. This could never happen. Not to the Divine Son of God Almighty. Could Jesus ever have asked His Heavenly Father to take away the very reason for which He came to this earth? Could Jesus ever make a statement questioning His trust in His Father? This could never happen.

What is your choice? To believe the reporting of man or believe in the Divine nature of the Son of God, Jesus. The purpose of this is not to bring criticism on scripture. The purpose of this is to increase your belief in Jesus. You as a Christian should have concern whenever hearing or reading anything that lessens the Divine Nature of Jesus the Christ.

WHAT IS KEEPING YOU FROM HEAVEN?

During the times of Jesus here on earth, there were people who did not believe in Resurrection and Salvation. Today there are many who still do not believe. Buddhist have control of millions of people. They do not believe in a Supreme Creator, Resurrection or Salvation. Buddhism is not a religion. It is a teaching of Buddha. There are many walking this earth who might as well call themselves Buddhist because their daily habits are the same. There is no God in their Lives.

Jesus said, no one comes to the Father but through Him. Many believe this statement means that you will be Saved only if you believe in Jesus. Is this what He said or only what we want to believe? Did Jesus ever say, you must believe in Me to be Saved? We must be careful not to read into scripture what we want it to say. Is Jesus actually simply saying that He will make the decision as to who comes to the Father? When we get to heaven, the only person we should be surprised to see is ourselves. Paul said that God forgave him because of his ignorance and unbelief. Even today, there are many who are too ignorant to believe in Jesus.

What is keeping you from heaven? Your lack of faith, the good life, quest for popularity. You came into this world with nothing and you will leave with nothing. Nothing material. There is something you will leave with that is not material. The love of God. He loved you before you came into this world and He will love you after leaving. Whatever it is that is keeping you from the JOY that is yours, pray that God will take it away. Only what you do for God will last. He created you from dust and to dust you shall return. While you are here, you have the opportunity to place your mark in the Book of Life.

To God be the Glory.

ATONEMENT

There is only one way to receive forgiveness for your sins, ask for it. What good does it do for a person to gain forgiveness and lose their Soul? Being forgiven does not mean that you will be Saved. You have to live the life you sing about in your song. Most people can sing a pretty song to God, but, too often it stops there. We have to walk our talk. God will not believe anything you tell Him. Living life in accordance to God's Will is a major part of the test. God knows that many humans are hypocrites. They say one thing but live another. Most people can do anything for a short period of time. Staying on the right road for a life time is what is difficult. Heaven can wait. God is not going to make it easy for you to get to heaven. The rewards are too great not to require sacrifice. God wants to know that you are for real. The atonement for sin that Jesus accomplished for us on the Cross is important beyond measure.

The benefits that comes to us as believers in Jesus are immeasurable. Because of the atonement of Jesus, sin can no longer separate us from God. The atonement of Jesus means that we cannot be negligent in our attitudes toward sin. Jesus suffered for us. We have the obligation to make sure His suffering is a benefit to all humanity.

YOUR RESURRECTED BODY

I once read a book about a man who was involved in a serious accident. He stated that he had, for a short period of time, died. He wrote of how he was received in heaven and his recognition of his family and friends who had passed away before him. Many people reading his statements would be in disbelief. Since medics were able to restore him to live, many would say that his accountings were all in his mind. Then we begin to read between the lines and get more meaning and understand from scripture. We remember how after the Resurrection of Jesus, Mary Magdalene and the disciples of Jesus recognized Him. Jesus said (I am for real). He permitted Thomas to touch Him and He showed His disciples His hands and feet. Jesus communicated three time with His disciples and give them the power of the Holy Spirit.

The Resurrected Body. We believers often wonder about life after death. Jesus said that He will return to bring Salvation to those who are waiting. After death, Jesus was Spirit, yet, others could recognize Him, talk to Him and touch Him. We have been informed that we will be transformed into the likeness of the body of Christ. This fresh and blood can never enter heaven. Jesus has told us that he who believes in Him shall live even after death. Many believe that Spirit cannot have a bodily form, yet, Jesus had a bodily form. Our bodies will be transformed in His likeness. The primary difference will be that our bodies will no longer require the needs and wants of this life. Our Resurrected bodies will be controlled by the Spirit. God will control our going out and our coming in. There will be no more night. They will not need the light of a lamp or the light of the sun, for the Lord God will give them light. And they will reign forever and ever.

MAMMON

Life is precious. For most people, there is nothing more precious. Our life or the life of another. We all know that we hold precious something that we will lose anyway. Yet, we cannot help ourselves. The quality of live. Longevity. Nothing is more important to most of us. We desire material wealth more than anything. Yet, there is nothing wrong with material wealth. There is nothing wrong with having a great deal of money. Money is not evil. The love of money is evil. The love of money turns into greed. We what to hold on to all that we have and we want more to hold on to.

There is only one entity that we should hold precious. God. The Creator of heaven and earth and everything in existence. We worship only God. Not money. Not even Jesus. Jesus gave God worship. We praise Jesus for His love, suffering, dying for us. He saved us. Before the sun rose, The Son Rose. The fact is that Jesus would be nothing without God. We would be nothing without God. We are imperfect people trying to serve a perfect God. Because of our imperfection, we may not always see the wisdom of God's plan, but, we must be obedient anyway. Only then will we receive the Grace of God. Grace is a gift permitting us to do what we could not otherwise do and permitting us to be what we could not otherwise be. Jesus is worthy of our praise. God is worthy of our worship. We give God the glory for the things He has done.

We give God the glory by the way we live. This is the only true way of giving God glory. We understand that mammon is not as important as our personal relationship with our families. We understand that the quality of life is found in love not in material wealth. One of the most precious gifts that God has given us is time. The way we share this gift with others determines our level of appreciation. The Lord giveth and the Lord taketh away. Blessed be the name of the Lord. The Lord gave us this time here on earth for two primary reasons. To glorify His name and to help others to live life more abundantly. We can only live life more abundantly by giving God the glory. Not the spirit of mammon, but the Spirit of God must be within us all.